PRAYER

THE HEART CHANGER
AND MOUNTAIN MOVER

By Lynnelle Pierce

Lynnelle Pierce
928 Sand Lake Drive
Zeeland, MI 49464
© 2003 Lynnelle Pierce

Cover Design: Michael A. Vander Wall
Cover Photographer: Nick de Vries
Editing: Martin and Kay Den Braber, Sharon Van Houten
Legal: William Dani

ABOUT THE AUTHOR

Lynnelle Pierce lives in Zeeland, Michigan, with her husband Tom. They have two married sons who are also in ministry.

Tom and Lynnelle travel extensively leading Bible studies, conferences, and seminars teaching the grace of God and the truths of His Word.

Lynnelle has written three other practical Bible study books:

Have You Heard About That Fruit?
God's Gals Haven't Changed a Bit!
What God Says, He Does!

You will discover that her books are written in a way that's understandable, straight forward, sincere, and 100% truthful. And that is exactly the way she wants it.

I dedicate this book to the Lord Jesus.

He is the only one who could have made prayer possible—
and He did!

TABLE OF CONTENTS

SPECIAL THANKS

A special thank you to:

...my family, who love me and believe in and support what the Lord's "mission" is for me,

...my friends who motivate and energize me, and

...Martin and Kay Den Braber, who have a God-given depth of understanding and ability to help me get my heart on paper.

You are all gifts to me from the Lord.

Dear Heavenly Father,

We come to praise Your holy Name. How majestic is Your Name in all the earth. The whole earth is filled with Your glory. We are in awe of who You are.

Thank You for granting us the undeserved privilege of coming into Your presence from wherever we are and whatever we are doing.

May You find our hearts filled with love for You, and may the overflow of our hearts produce actions that please You and fulfill the mission You have ordained for us.

Father, we are sinners, and our sins hurt You so. We pray for Your forgiveness and cleansing. How lost we would be without Your grace! Words cannot thank You enough, so may our lives of service demonstrate our gratitude.

Lord, God, my personal petition is that this book will be not just mere words on a page, but rather a learning tool that You use to teach all of us how much You love to communicate with Your children.

We open ourselves up to Your teaching through the power of Your sweet Holy Spirit.

In Jesus' Name,
Amen.

1

WHY PRAY?

Prayer. The mere thought and sound of that word brings comfort, serenity, and peace. According to Webster, prayer is a spiritual communion with God, as in adoration, confession, thanksgiving, and supplication. It may include a devout petition.[1] But even more than that, prayer connects us to the one and only God, and it makes us powerfully aware of His presence in our lives.

Prayer is certainly a very familiar word in the religious community. We understand that prayer is a vital and essential element in a rewarding spiritual journey. But, unfortunately, if we are brutally honest, it has become sadly apparent that personal daily prayer time with Almighty God has become dangerously absent, or at best, terribly infrequent in the priorities chosen for everyday living by far too many of us.

The failure to properly prioritize our prayer time may be the result of dealing with a packed full daily schedule of activities, responsibilities, and pressures that this life throws at us. Or it may be the result of confusion from a misunderstood past prayer experience. Or maybe it is because of discouragement from the feeling that personal prayer time is not providing the comfort, serenity, and peace that God's Word has promised. I believe that when we are faced with those types of circumstances, the part of our human nature that demands to be in control rises up and we think that we can handle life in our way—on our own terms. Doesn't that sound horrible? It is!

However, there is a Book available to us to inspire our spiritual nature to take charge of choosing the proper priority for our personal <u>daily</u> prayer time. I know, and can joyfully testify, that God's Word has all the answers needed to inspire us to give our daily personal prayer time a jump start, moving us in the <u>right</u> direction on our spiritual journey.

Won't you join with me in this study of prayer as we, together with the Holy Spirit as our guide, seek out God's divine wisdom, direction, and inspiration that can only be discovered in His Holy Word?

Let's first open our Bibles to 2 Chronicles 7:14 where we discover:

> "...if my people, who are called by my name, will humble themselves and pray and seek my face and turn from their wicked ways, then will I hear from heaven and will forgive their sin and will heal their land."

Did you take note of the part of that verse that states, *if my people...will* <u>humble themselves</u> *and pray* (emphasis mine)? Humble ourselves! That requirement makes praying an unnatural activity, for to humble ourselves goes against the very grain of our proud human nature. We all love to think that we can handle all the circumstances we encounter and fix all the broken pieces in our lives. But by praying, we are admitting we don't have all the answers to deal with all the circumstances we encounter, nor do we have the necessary tools to fix all the broken pieces in our journey down life's highways and byways. Haven't we all been down those roads?

Prayer is so much more than simply closing our eyes, folding our hands, and starting the "asking for" process. It's genuinely connecting our spirit to the one and only Holy Spirit—the Spirit of God Himself. (Isn't that awesome!) It's

"Be still, and know that I am God" (Psalm 46:10a). We have to slow down to pray. Most of us are far too busy expending our energies just getting through each day's schedule to maintain an energized spiritual life. Where does that *still small voice* fit into our hectic lives? If we can hear it, that's the Voice that will lead and guide us.

> *And he said, Go forth, and stand upon the mount before the Lord. And, behold, the Lord passed by, and a great and strong wind rent the mountains, and brake in pieces the rocks before the Lord; but the Lord was not in the wind: and after the wind an earthquake; but the Lord was not in the earthquake: And after the earthquake a fire; but the Lord was not in the fire: and after the fire a still small voice* (1 Kings 19:11-12 KJV).

Let's be quiet, slow down, and listen to what He wants to say to us.

Prayer is not a means to get ahold of what we want, but instead it is to get ahold of Him. We need that intimate communication with God; it revitalizes our spiritual lives and makes our relationships with the Lord more real and meaningful. The more we experience that intimacy and open our lives to personal prayer with Him, the more we recognize prayer's power source—God.

And the more we acknowledge His power, the more we realize we cannot handle life on our own (which He never intended anyway).

> *Let us then approach the throne of grace with confidence, so that we may receive mercy and*

find grace to help us in our time of need
(Hebrews 4:16).

In addition to admitting we cannot handle life on our own, we need to acknowledge that we cannot approach His throne on our own either. Again I say, prayer is connecting with God—spiritually being in His very presence. That is only possible when we've been washed with the saving blood of Jesus, our Savior, thereby wearing the proper clothing—the white robe of His righteousness.

> *I delight greatly in the Lord; my soul rejoices in my God. For he has clothed me with garments of salvation and arrayed me in a robe of righteousness, as a bridegroom adorns his head like a priest, and as a bride adorns herself with her jewels* (Isaiah 61:10).

God loves us so much that even though we are sinners—undeserving of His love—God desired to make us right again, take away our sins, and give us the proper attire of righteousness to permit us to have a deep and exciting personal relationship with Him. Paul describes all of us in Romans 3:23:

> *...for all have sinned and fall short of the glory of God....*

Therefore, we all need a Savior, and the greatest joy in all of Christianity is that we have one—Jesus!

> *"Salvation is found in no one else, for there is no other name under heaven given to men by which we must be saved"* (Acts 4:12).

What it cost God to give us our Savior is truly mind-boggling. God sent His only Son to be the ultimate sacrifice. Jesus burdened Himself with <u>all</u> of <u>our</u> sins (He is sinless) when they nailed Him to the cross at Calvary. He literally took our place. We deserved to be crucified, but Jesus said in John 3:16,

"For God so loved the world that he gave his one and only Son, that whoever believes in him shall not perish but have eternal life."

That love-filled verse is monumental for our lives when we truly believe those words with our hearts and accept Jesus as our personal Lord and Savior. Only then can we share with Him His victory over death, and in praise and adoration join with Him in our brand new resurrected eternal life! That new life is continuously fed and nurtured by God's Spirit when we humbly present ourselves at His throne through prayer.

Remember the one and only Almighty God desires and invites us to spend time with Him.

pray continually; (1 Thessalonians 5:17).

I want men everywhere to lift up holy hands in prayer, without anger or disputing (1 Tim. 2:8).

For we do not have a high priest who is unable to sympathize with our weaknesses, but we have one who has been tempted in every way, just as we are—yet was without sin (Hebrews 4:15).

He's interested. He understands. He loves us and wants us to stay close to Him, and He's given us the gift of prayer to prove it. So let's use it.

*The Lord is near to all who call on him, to all
who call on him in truth* (Psalm 145:18).

What does it mean to call on Him in truth? In our
relationship with God, it is vital for us to understand and accept
the fact that God knows our hearts. We cannot successfully
disguise, distort, or lie about our true feelings when we pray to
God. Our verbal skills may be polished from years of practice in
attempting to mask our true feelings by playing word games
with others. But God is not dependent upon carefully chosen
words that come from our lips to decipher what is in our
thoughts and hearts. In Psalm 139: 2 and 4, the psalmist David
writes,

*You know when I sit and when I rise; you
perceive my thoughts from afar* (v.2).

*Before a word is on my tongue you know it
completely, O Lord* (v.4).

And from 1 Samuel 16:7b, it is revealed to us,

*"The Lord does not look at the things man looks
at. Man looks at the outward appearance, but the
Lord looks at the heart."*

It is very clear from those verses that we cannot hide the
truth from God. But then again, why would we even try to when
He promised to be *near to all who call on him in truth?*
In addition, it is also vital in our relationship with God
to recognize whom we are calling upon with our truth. We have
the honor and privilege, through prayer, to call upon the very
foundation of Divine Truth. Scripture describes the Truth as
being in God the Father, God the Son, God the Holy Spirit, and
God's Holy Word.

...a faith and knowledge resting on the hope of eternal life, which God, who does not lie, promised before the beginning of time,... (Titus 1:2).

Jesus answered, "I am the way and the truth and the life" (John 14:6a).

"When the Counselor comes, whom I will send to you from the Father, the Spirit of truth who goes out from the Father, he will testify about me" (John 15:26).

All Scripture is God-breathed ...(2 Tim. 3:16a).

I think we are at a very good point in our study of prayer where I would like to get down to the heart of the matter of the true spiritual condition of your heart. Have you really experienced His presence? Or could it be that everything you have just read did not connect with your mind or touch your heart? Could it be you didn't understand that prayer is a gift for only the "born again" believer in Christ Jesus? I have good news for you! The first prayer from our heart that God hears is our prayer of confession. You see, it doesn't have to be complicated. You can have Jesus' very Spirit living inside your heart, making understanding possible. Simply profess Jesus as your only Savior, ask Him to live in your heart, repent of your sins, and let Him help you change your ways (He's been waiting to hear from you). How exciting to read this in 2 Corinthians 5:17,

Therefore, if anyone is in Christ, he is a new creation; the old has gone, the new has come!

Believe that Jesus' death and resurrection were for YOU, and then you will receive His Holy Spirit. Watch a new you unfold!

Now it is God who makes both us and you stand firm in Christ. He anointed us, set his seal of ownership on us, and put his Spirit in our hearts as a deposit, guaranteeing what is to come (2 Corinthians 1:21-22).

And for those of you who already have His seal of ownership on you and His Spirit living in your heart, I would also ask each one of you to take a look deep within yourself. And when you do, truthfully answer this question: "Have I been giving only lip service to the Lord in prayer, or am I pouring out my heartfelt feelings and emotions to Him?" Remember, He sees your heart and perceives your thoughts. If you have been holding yourself back because you do not have God in His proper place in your life or do not have a full understanding of who He really is, listen to the prophet Isaiah as we continue on in our study.

In the year that King Uzziah died, I saw the Lord seated on a throne, high and exalted, and the train of his robe filled the temple. Above him were seraphs, each with six wings: With two wings they covered their faces, with two they covered their feet, and with two they were flying. And they were calling to one another: "Holy, holy, holy is the Lord Almighty; the whole earth is full of his glory." At the sound of their voices the doorposts and thresholds shook and the temple was filled with smoke (Isaiah 6:1-4).

Who has measured the waters in the hollow of his hand, or with the breadth of his hand marked off the heavens? Who has held the dust of the earth in a basket, or weighed the mountains on the scales and the hills in a balance?

Lift your eyes and look to the heavens: Who created all these? He who brings out the starry host one by one, and calls them each by name. Because of his great power and mighty strength, not one of them is missing (Isaiah 40:12, 26).

"I am the Lord, and there is no other; apart from me there is no God" (Isaiah 45:5a).

WOW! And that same God wants to be connected to us and to be interacting in every detail of our day-to-day living. When our lives are spiritually fixed on Him we begin to see with new insight that: He's big! He's powerful! He's majestic! He's the blessed controller of all things—even you and me! Yes, He's able!

He who dwells in the shelter of the Most High will rest in the shadow of the Almighty. I will say of the Lord, "He is my refuge and my fortress, my God, in whom I trust" (Psalm 91:1-2).

Yes! Yes! Yes!

He is able to do immeasurably more than we could ask or imagine (from Ephesians 3:20). There is great strength in the name of the Lord. What an awesome God! How easy it should be to keep our lives spiritually fixed on Him. Why then does our human nature find it so difficult, indeed, to stay focused on Him? Here is where the rubber meets the road—humanity meets

Divinity. Human nature is not grounded in Divinity, but conceived in sin. Sadly, it doesn't take very much effort at all for our sinful human nature to overwhelm our wholesome thoughts, constructive deeds, and good intentions, and turn them into anything but.

As it is written: "There is no one righteous, not even one; there is no one who understands, no one who seeks God. All have turned away, they have together become worthless; there is no one who does good, not even one" (Romans 3:10-12).

What are the factors that show up in our sinful nature that make it so difficult for us to do good and to be good? There are certainly many. I have listed just some of them on this page for your review and consideration.

Unfortunately, these factors blend naturally with our fallen human condition. So we revert to them easily and quickly. So easily and quickly, in fact, that we find ourselves depending upon our built-in protective layers of self-deception to falsely rationalize our sinful actions, words, and deeds. Do these examples sound familiar?

Some Factors That Fuel Our Sinful Human Nature

Anger
Anxiety
Depression
Environments of
   abusiveness
   permissiveness
   oppression
Envy
Hidden agendas
Indecision
Inferiority complex
Jealousy
Poor family relationships
Prejudice
Pride
Rationalizing
Repression
Revengefulness
Self-deception
Superiority complex
Unforgiving spirit
Unhealthy fear
Victim mentality
Vindictiveness

1)   "Everybody does it, so why shouldn't I?"
2)   "It's not like it's a crime or something!"
3)   "What I did wasn't half as bad as what they did."
4)   "They don't deserve my help."
5)   "They had it coming to them."
6)   "I'll teach them a lesson they'll never forget!"

Take heart, all is not lost. We can choose to bring the focus of our lives back to that royal throne Isaiah saw. We need to get our hearts persuaded in the scriptural truth that nothing is too difficult for our God to handle. He has just been waiting for us to acknowledge His power and humbly seek His help.

But now a righteousness from God, apart from law, has been made known, to which the Law and the Prophets testify. This righteousness from God comes through faith in Jesus Christ to all who believe (Romans 3:21-22a).

Now let's compare our outlook and tone generated from our human righteousness in the six examples above to our outlook and tone when we receive God's righteousness through faith in Christ Jesus:

1)   "Just because everybody does it, it doesn't make it right."
2)   "It may not be a crime, but I know that God doesn't approve—so count me out."
3)   "Two wrongs don't make a right."
4)   "How may I be of service to you?"
5)   "Who am I to judge?"
6)   "If I don't forgive men when they sin against me, God will not forgive my sins." (See Matthew 6: 14-15).

What a difference! We need to seek His righteousness through prayer. And making our prayers effective boils down to, in large part, learning how great He is. How do we do that? We need to study the Book He wrote for us and look at His magnificent creation.

I have a friend who is the mother of a beautiful special needs child. This little girl took one look at the sunrise one morning and said to her mommy, "God sure did a good job!" God did create the heavens and the earth, and it was good (see Genesis 1).

As we ponder His awesome creation and study His Holy Word, all of our misunderstanding, confusion, and discouragement about the effectiveness of our prayer lives should quickly fade away. But wait a minute. No more misunderstanding, confusion, or discouragement? That doesn't sound like an accurate description of the world we live in, does it?

There are hurdles to clear to avoid misunderstanding just how difficult it is to maintain an effective prayer life. Those hurdles are called prayer demolishers. Could it be that you are currently not even praying because your life is filled with prayer demolishers? For instance, unconfessed/unforgiven sin. Unconfessed sin is simply sin that you have been convicted of, but you're not doing anything about it. Remember, sin is still sin, even if you haven't "been caught" yet. God knows, even when others don't. This one stops prayer immediately simply because we cannot get into God's presence with convicting, unconfessed, and unforgiven sin; it separates us from God, so it stands to reason that our prayers are blocked from reaching Him.

If I had cherished sin in my heart, the Lord would not have listened; (Psalm 66:18).

However, you can defeat the unconfessed/unforgiven sin prayer demolisher with a prayer of repentance.

Then I acknowledged my sin to you and did not cover up my iniquity. I said, "I will confess my transgressions to the Lord"—and you forgave the guilt of my sin (Psalm 32:5).

Be on guard for other prayer demolishers like hostility and an unforgiving spirit. They are like acids which eat away at our desire to pray. In addition, please add these dangerous prayer demolishers to your watch out for list:

selfishness (rather than for God's honor, glory, and purpose),

When you ask, you do not receive, because you ask with wrong motives, that you may spend what you get on your pleasures (James 4:3).

an uncaring attitude,

If a man shuts his ears to the cry of the poor, he too will cry out and not be answered (Proverbs 21:13).

and inadequate faith.

If any of you lacks wisdom, he should ask God, who gives generously to all without finding fault, and it will be given to him. But when he asks, he must believe and not doubt, because he who doubts is like a wave of the sea, blown and tossed by the wind. That man should not think he will receive anything from the Lord; he is a double-minded man, unstable in all he does (James 1:5-8).

After dealing with prayer demolishers, we need to address the confusion that comes from the question of unanswered prayer. "He doesn't answer anyway." Has that thought ever crossed your mind? That thought may be a direct result of exactly what and how you are asking. Sometimes our requests are out of sync with God's timing. Take Peter's suggestion in Matthew 17:1-5, for example,

> *After six days Jesus took with him Peter, James and John the brother of James, and led them up a high mountain by themselves. There he was transfigured before them. His face shown like the sun, and his clothes became as white as the light. Just then there appeared before them Moses and Elijah, talking with Jesus. Peter said to Jesus, "Lord it is good for us to be here. If you wish, I will put up three shelters—one for you, one for Moses, and one for Elijah."*
> *While he was still speaking, a bright cloud enveloped them, and a voice from the cloud said, "This is my Son, whom I love; with him I am well pleased. Listen to him!"*

At that moment, it sounded like a fabulous idea to Peter. But then Jesus would not have gone to the cross, and we would not have a Savior. Fortunately, God loves us too much to say "Yes" to our requests when they are not in His ultimate plan (though we don't always understand that at the time).

We need to guard against discouragement when we are faced with what we feel is unanswered prayer. We need to consider that what we perceive as unanswered prayer could be a

"Not yet" answer, or even a "No" answer from God. We are so conditioned to want our request responded to right <u>NOW</u>. God has His reasons for "Not yet" or "No." If we are willing to wait for the "Not yet" to materialize and not force a human solution, He can build character, endurance, trust, patience, and submission during the waiting period. Not bad, huh? A lot of spiritual gain can come from His "Not yet." And as relates to God saying "No" to our requests, I can tell you, as I look back over my prayer life experiences with God, I find myself very thankful that God loved me enough to say "No, my child" many times. If you don't accept His answer, you will not only miss His best, you may suffer short or long-term consequences as a result of your substituted misguided solution. So don't get discouraged. Our Father knows best.

> *Oh, the depth of the riches of the wisdom and knowledge of God! How unsearchable his judgments, and his paths beyond tracing out!*
> *"Who has known the mind of the Lord? Or who has been his counselor?" "Who has ever given to God, that God should repay him?" For from him and through him and to him are all things. To him be the glory forever! Amen* (Romans 11:33-36).

The gift of prayer—truly a personal audience with the King of kings. That's why we pray!

LESSON 1
WHY PRAY?

1. What is prayer?

2. What keeps prayer from being your top priority? What could change that?

3. From 2 Chronicles 7:14, why is humility a critical requirement?

4. How does the Lord speak to you? How do you hear Him?

5. Read Psalm 46:10. Why is that an all-important factor to prayer? What happens when you listen?

6. What is the proper attire in God's presence? (Isaiah 61:10.)

7. What does John 3:16 mean to you personally?

8. How do you know that God wants to spend time with you?

9. How much does God understand you and your particular request and need? (Hebrews 4:15-16; Psalm 139:2-4.)

10. What is truth?

11. What is the first "prayer" the Lord hears from us? Explain.

12. What is Isaiah's view of God? How can Isaiah's view be
     your view? Why will that motivate your prayer life?

13. What factors fuel our sinful human nature? Why do you
     think that's true?

14. What are prayer demolishers? Be specific.

15. Why does it seem your prayers are not answered?

2

LEARNING FROM THE BEST

When it comes to prayer, it seems like we constantly need to be reassured that God is really listening. Oh, He is!

> *The eyes of the Lord are on the righteous and his ears are attentive to their cry; the face of the Lord is against those who do evil, to cut off the memory of them from the earth.*
> *The righteous cry out, and the Lord hears them; he delivers them from all their troubles* (Psalm 34:15–17).

We also need to be confident of the fact that He'll answer our prayers. What may disturb us is that down deep we know that God might not answer the way we think He should. Hear the word of the Lord:

> *"For my thoughts are not your thoughts, neither are your ways my ways," declares the Lord. "As the heavens are higher than the earth, so are my ways higher than your ways and my thoughts than your thoughts"* (Isaiah 55:8-9).

God has three ways He answers prayer: "Yes," "No," and "Not yet." Truly believing that He has our best interests in mind is the only way we're going to accept the answers He has for us—especially when it's "No" or "Not yet." And please note that even when the answer is "Yes," when based on our human expectations, sometimes the results turn out very different than we planned on or anticipated. (Sound familiar?)

Truly believing with our hearts takes faith. Prayer takes faith—believing that God hears, answers, is able, and also knows what is best. Faith is believing that prayer makes a difference. Faith is a deep trust in the Lord, even when you don't understand or you can't see any positive outcome. Faith is knowing God and knowing God has a plan.

When you don't understand,
When you don't see His plan,
When you can't trace His hand,
Trust His heart![2]

Faith is also choosing to trust what God has promised.

Now faith is being sure of what we hope for and certain of what we do not see (Hebrews 11:1).

And we know that in all things God works for the good of those who love him, who have been called according to his purpose (Romans 8:28).

Keep your lives free from the love of money and be content with what you have, because God has said, "Never will I leave you; never will I forsake you" (Hebrews 13:5).

"For I know the plans I have for you," declares the Lord, "plans to prosper you and not to harm you, plans to give you hope and a future. Then you will call upon me and come and pray to me,

and I will listen to you. You will seek me and find me when you seek me with all your heart" (Jeremiah 29:11-13).

Seeking the Lord with all His heart was exactly the way Jesus called upon the Lord in prayer. Jesus' prayer life was, without a doubt, our ultimate example of how we should approach the Lord in prayer. He is the Son of God, sent to earth on a mission—to be the Savior of the world. Even though Jesus is fully God, He still knew how desperately He needed to connect with and stay connected to His Father during His earthly pilgrimage.

Immediately Jesus made the disciples get into the boat and go on ahead of him to the other side, while he dismissed the crowd. After he had dismissed them, he went up on a mountainside by himself to pray. When evening came, he was there alone,...(Matthew 14:22-23).

One of those days Jesus went out to a mountainside to pray, and spent the night praying to God (Luke 6:12).

Jesus is also the Son of Man, meaning that He has personally experienced this world's trials, temptations, and influence. So during His time on earth He also needed to get away from the pressures of everyday life, people, and their expectations of Him. By connecting with His Father through prayer, He received encouragement and direction. He felt an infusion of power and strength. The Father was the source of that power and strength, the law of His life, and His inspiration. He received all of that through faith-based prayer. In order to complete the mission His Father sent Him to do, Jesus knew He needed prayer; and if He did, we certainly do.

We went on a mission trip years ago to a very poor part of the world. Conditions were not at all the way we were used to. We had gotten spoiled and soft. At first, the poverty, the dirt, and the cockroaches (bigger than I've ever seen before) were all we could see. It was an understatement to say that I wanted to go home. If I'd had my way, that's exactly what I would have done. But I couldn't. So, my husband Tom, our son Jason, and I held a small, but powerful, prayer meeting. We prayed that our eyes would not focus on the physical, but that we would be able to see the people through the eyes of Jesus with His purpose in mind. What a miraculous change! It had to be a miracle, because I didn't even react to ants on my toothbrush or a lizard in my towel. Only God can do that! Prayer changed our focus from the physical surroundings to the spiritual needs of the people, and the mission was accomplished victoriously.

God has a mission assignment for all of us. For you see, before time began, God ordained (pre-determined) every day of our lives. To know His mission for us and to stay committed to it, we need to connect through prayer with the One who knows the mission plan absolutely perfectly. We simply cannot miss any of the details when we stay connected to Him in faith-based prayer and seek His perfect individualized direction.

Just like the prayers of Jesus, our faith-based prayers will reach the Father's power and strength through Christ, who is our inspiration and in whom we discover abundant life.

In Matthew 6:9-13, Jesus gives us a model prayer—one after which to pattern all our prayers. It's called "The Lord's Prayer." Jesus said,

"This, then, is how you should pray:

> *"'Our Father in heaven,*
> *hallowed be your name,*
> *your kingdom come,*
> *your will be done on earth as it is in heaven.*
> *Give us today our daily bread.*
> *Forgive us our debts, as we also have forgiven our*
> *debtors.*
> *And lead us not into temptation,*
> *but deliver us from the evil one.'"*

Many of us know this prayer practically backward and forward. But, if we specifically break down the various parts of this prayer, we can see why this is such a wonderful formula for prayer. So, let's get specific.

Our Father: When we start this way, it automatically and immediately reminds us of just who we are praying to. He is our heavenly Father, meaning that we are His children. He loves us with an unexplainable love. Because of the sacrifice of Jesus, we belong to the tightly knit family of God. And what a family that is!

> *For this reason I kneel before the Father, from*
> *whom his whole family in heaven and on earth*
> *derives its name* (Ephesians 3:14-15).

In heaven: Our prayers ascend to heaven, where God the Father oversees all from His royal throne. Our Father is sovereign, majestic, omnipotent, and omnipresent. For Him nothing is too difficult; He is over all, in all, and through all. He is the mountain mover. (Life's problems sometimes look like immovable mountains.)

> *Jesus replied, "I tell you the truth, if you have*
> *faith and do not doubt, not only can you do what*

was done to the fig tree, but also you can say to this mountain, 'Go, throw yourself into the sea,' and it will be done. If you believe, you will receive whatever you ask for in prayer" (Matthew 21:21-22).

God is not a sugar daddy, waiting to give us everything we want. Many of us want what we don't need and need what we don't want. God has promised to move our mountains and supply our needs. He knows just what to do, and when and how to do it, because He is God—we're not.

"...then from heaven, your dwelling place, hear their prayer and their plea, and uphold their cause" (1 Kings 8:49).

Heaven is God's dwelling place; that's what makes it heaven!

Hallowed [holy] *be your name:* This is the time in our prayer when God wants our worship and praise because of who He is. This is such a vital time because it causes us to forget about ourselves and totally concentrate on Him and give Him what He so deserves—true glory, honor, and praise. He is worthy!

I come from a very conservative Dutch background, for which I am grateful in many ways. However, if I am not careful, that influence can also be rather stifling and bound with legalism. But I had an extraordinary experience in our church one Sunday morning. We sang one of my favorite hymns, "It is Well With My Soul."[3] I totally got into the meaning of that song, especially the line that spoke of, "my sin not in part but the whole, Is nailed to the cross and I bear it no more, Praise the Lord, praise the Lord, Oh my soul!" Without even realizing it, my hand reached up as if to touch the face of God and say thank you. It was a moment I'll never forget. The Lord loves our praise, and we should love to give it to Him. Holy is the Lord.

Your kingdom come, your will be done on earth as it is in heaven: The Lord wants us to surrender our lives to Him daily. We are, by sinful human nature, absorbed with ourselves. Jesus reminds us that to be a true follower of His, we are to deny ourselves.

> *Jesus turned and said to Peter, "Get behind me, Satan! You are a stumbling block to me; you do not have in mind the things of God, but the things of men"* (Matthew 16:23).

> *Then he said to them all: "If anyone would come after me, he must deny himself and take up his cross daily and follow me"* (Luke 9:23).

We are also to submit our wills to God and totally desire His will.

> *Therefore, I urge you, brothers, in view of God's mercy, to offer your bodies as living sacrifices, holy and pleasing to God—this is your spiritual act of worship. Do not conform any longer to the pattern of this world, but be transformed by the renewing of your mind. Then you will be able to test and approve what God's will is—his good, pleasing and perfect will* (Romans 12:1-2).

The result is beautiful satisfaction and contentment.

Give us today our daily bread: This part is so much more than just food. Yes, we need daily physical food, but we need daily nourishment for three other areas of our lives as well: emotional, mental, and spiritual.

It is here where we lay our daily concerns and needs before Him because He said we could.

> *Cast all your anxiety on him because he cares for you* (1 Peter 5:7).

Because our daily lives affect these four areas of our beings, we need to ask Him for a daily balanced supply of nourishment to sustain us from day to day for whatever that particular day holds. Remember, Jesus is the bread of life!

> *"I am the bread of life. Your forefathers ate the manna in the desert, yet they died. But here is the bread that comes down from heaven, which a man may eat and not die. I am the living bread that came down from heaven. If anyone eats of this bread, he will live forever. This bread is my flesh, which I will give for the life of the world"* (John 6:48-51).

Forgive us our debts, as we also have forgiven our debtors: A day should never go by that we do not take a good look at the sins we have just committed and sincerely repent from and receive forgiveness for them.

> *If we confess our sins, he is faithful and just and will forgive us our sins and purify us from all unrighteousness* (1 John 1:9).

Praise the Lord! Aren't you grateful He'll do that for you? That is exactly what He wants us to do to others who have done something against us. An unforgiving spirit, even if you feel justified in having it, is like a heavy albatross that burdens you down with feelings of bitterness, hatred, and destruction.

That's why Jesus says to get rid of our burdens daily. Forgiveness does not mean that the person you have forgiven is getting away with anything, but rather, that you're handing the whole ordeal over to the Lord, allowing Him to deal with it in His perfect way, setting you free!

> *When they hurled their insults at him, he did not retaliate; when he suffered, he made no threats. Instead, he entrusted himself to him who judges justly* (1 Peter 2:23).

And lead us not into temptation, but deliver us from the evil one: God tests us because He loves us and wants us to spiritually "grow up" and mature in our faith in Him, but He would never tempt us or lead us into evil.

> *When tempted, no one should say, "God is tempting me." For God cannot be tempted by evil, nor does he tempt anyone;* (James 1:13).

We have an enemy—actually, a couple of them. One of them is the evil one, and we blame him for everything we do wrong—Satan. He's the deceiver. He camouflages as the angel of light. He prowls around to see whom he can devour. However, while all of that is true, he can't make us sin. Hear what James tells us in James 1:4,

> *Perseverance must finish its work so that you may be mature and complete, not lacking anything.*

Satan can make sin look mighty good and tasty, but we have no one to blame but ourselves for taking a big bite out of the bait. So, I think <u>we</u> are our own worst enemy. God's power is far greater than Satan's or our own. If we stay connected to God through prayer, not only will we be empowered in our daily struggles to fight off sin, but also to help resist temptation.

> *No temptation has seized you except what is common to man. And God is faithful; he will not let you be tempted beyond what you can bear. But when you are tempted, he will also provide a way out so that you can stand up under it* (1 Corinthians 10:13).

Hallelujah! Amen! Let it be so!

Jesus lets us listen in to another of His precious prayer examples in the book of John. In John 17:1, Jesus prayed for Himself. He then prayed for His disciples who were the closest to Him (17:11), and then He prayed for all believers (17:23).

> *After Jesus said this, he looked toward heaven and prayed: "Father, the time has come. Glorify your Son, that your Son may glorify you"* (John 17:1).

> *"I will remain in the world no longer, but they are still in the world, and I am coming to you. Holy Father, protect them by the power of your name—the name you gave me—so that they may be one as we are one"* (John 17:11).

> *"I in them and you in me. May they be brought to complete unity to let the world know that you sent me and have loved them even as you have loved me"* (John 17:23).

There is such a beautiful order to His prayer that makes perfect sense. Each one of us must personally connect ourselves with the Lord so that He can change us first. We cannot take anyone farther than where we are ourselves. It goes like this: I desire to get my life right with the Lord so that He, living in me, overflows and affects the ones closest to me—and then, after the change in us, we can together affect our neighbors, our community, and our world. Revival begins when His Spirit comes to live individually within each and every one of us. Allow the Lord to revive you, which in turn can affect the people around you, and which then can change our world.

Jesus came to change the world and certainly encountered the worst it had to offer. Before Jesus faced the worst of times, He needed to grab ahold of and hang onto His Father. In Matthew 3, Jesus felt the strength and approval from His Father, which gave Jesus what He needed to face Satan when He was physically weak (Matthew 4:1-11).

As soon as Jesus was baptized, he went up out of the water. At that moment heaven was opened, and he saw the Spirit of God descending like a dove and lighting on him. And a voice from heaven said, "This is my Son, whom I love; with him I am well pleased." (Matthew 3:16-17).

He also held tight to His Father's love, knowing that soon He would be facing the cross. Prayer was His access (and is also ours) to the Father, who is the power source, which enabled Him to face what was ahead.

While he was still speaking, a bright cloud enveloped them, and a voice from the cloud said, "This is my Son, whom I love; with him I am well pleased. Listen to him!" (Matthew 17:5).

"So do not fear, for I am with you; do not be dismayed, for I am your God. I will strengthen you and help you; I will uphold you with my righteous right hand" (Isaiah 41:10).

The apostle Paul tells us to never stop praying. Jesus never stopped, and we can't afford to either. We can't live life to the fullest without Him—that's for sure.

pray continually; (1 Thessalonians 5:17).

"...apart from me you can do nothing" (John 15:5b).

Have you ever wondered how Jesus could do it? How could He know His mission to the last deadly detail and still go through with it?

Who, being in very nature God, did not consider equality with God something to be grasped, but made himself nothing, taking the very nature of a servant, being made in human likeness. And being found in appearance as a man, he humbled himself and became obedient to death—even death on a cross! (Philippians 2:6-8).

He demonstrated His true heartfelt feelings in Mark 14:32-42:

They went to a place called Gethsemane, and Jesus said to his disciples, "Sit here while I pray." He took Peter, James and John along with him, and he began to be deeply distressed and troubled. "My soul is overwhelmed with

> sorrow to the point of death," he said to them. "Stay here and keep watch."
>
> Going a little farther, he fell to the ground and prayed that if possible the hour might pass from him. "Abba, Father," he said, "everything is possible for you. Take this cup from me. Yet not what I will, but what you will."
>
> Then he returned to his disciples and found them sleeping. "Simon," he said to Peter, "are you asleep? Could you not keep watch for one hour? Watch and pray so that you will not fall into temptation. The spirit is willing, but the body is weak."
>
> Once more he went away and prayed the same thing. When he came back, he again found them sleeping, because their eyes were heavy. They did not know what to say to him.
>
> Returning the third time, he said to them, "Are you still sleeping and resting? Enough! The hour has come. Look, the Son of Man is betrayed into the hands of sinners. Rise! Let us go! Here comes my betrayer!"

He was deeply distressed and troubled. If there was any other way God's salvation plan could be worked out, He was game. Yet He surrendered His will over to His Father's will. He stopped trying to control the circumstances He found himself in and was willing to obey His Father's will. Oh, the power of faith-based prayer is an understatement here.

Our will has to be surrendered to His, and our faith in the One we pray to has to be bigger than our feelings. Jesus demonstrated that there isn't anyone, even Himself, who enjoys facing difficult times. But by His example we learn from the

Best that when we <u>choose</u> to plug into our prayer power source—God, He will give us what it takes.

Thank you, Jesus, for our lessons in prayer.

LESSON 2

LEARNING FROM THE BEST

1. What aspects of prayer would you most like reassurance about?

2. What is faith? Does prayer take faith? Explain your answer. (Isaiah 55:8-9.)

3. Read Matthew 14:23. Why did Jesus go by Himself to pray so many times during His earthly ministry? What can we learn from that?

4. Read Matthew 6:9-13. Why is the Lord's Prayer a model prayer for you? Highlight each point.

5. For whom and for what does Jesus pray in John 17:1-5? In verses 17:6-19? In verses 17:20-26? Be very specific. What lessons are there for you in this prayer?

6. Many times the Lord uses prayer to encourage you because when you pray you feel so close to Him. Read Matthew 3:16-17; 17:5. Why did Jesus need to feel especially close to His Father at these two particular times?

7. How often should you pray? (1Thessalonians 5:17.)

8. Read Mark 14:32-42. What feelings did Jesus express in this prayer?

9.   Why did Jesus want Peter, James, and John along with Him?

10.   Jesus spoke specifically to Simon Peter in Mark 14:37-38. Why? How can prayer keep us from temptation?

11.   Knowing that prayer is a sure connection with God and is more than just asking for things, according to James 5:13 when are two important times to pray? How can you pray "praise"?

12.   What keeps you from a powerful prayer life? What does it take to have a powerful prayer life?

3

PRAYING FOR GOD'S WILL

Have you ever wondered if prayer really changes anything? If God has His plans and will work out His purposes, do we really need to pray? Simple, pat answers to questions like those are impossible. However, as we discovered from our study in chapters 1 and 2, the Bible does tell us to pray. Prayer is a very intimate way to have two-way communication with God. It's the way our relationship with God deepens and gets to be more personal. So, yes, we need to pray. Can we change God's mind? We cannot possibly understand the infinite mind of Almighty God with finite human minds (as great as they may be). But the prayers of His children do please Him.

> *...but the prayer of the upright pleases him* (Proverbs 15:8b).

So let's continue to pray, and let God be God.

As God, He sets up His rules, not to be difficult, but because He loves us and wants us living in His will for our lives. Without guidelines and structure, there is chaos and disorder. He desires that we obey Him. Read what God said to the people of Israel in Exodus 19: 4-5a:

> *"'You yourselves have seen what I did to Egypt, and how I carried you on eagles' wings and brought you to myself. Now if you obey me fully*

and keep my covenant, then out of all nations
you will be my treasured possession....'"

"They will be mine," says the Lord Almighty,
"in the day when I make up my treasured
possession. I will spare them, just as in
compassion a man spares his son who serves
him. And you will again see the distinction
between the righteous and the wicked, between
those who serve God and those who do not"
(Malachi 3:17-18).

As His treasured possessions, we should desire to obey
His will. But we need to understand that when we don't, we
may experience the wrath of God.

Therefore I will make the heavens tremble; and
the earth will shake from its place at the wrath
of the Lord Almighty, in the day of his burning
anger (Isaiah 13:13).

Since we have now been justified by his blood,
how much more shall we be saved from God's
wrath through him! (Romans 5:9.)

We don't like to talk or even think about God's wrath.
But it is real, and He can come down hard when we disobey. As
with any parent-child relationship, children do not like to
experience wrath and punishment, but they have to realize that
disobedience reaps consequences. Make no mistake here, there
is a final destruction for the unrepentant heart—hell. Lessons
must be learned. Lives have to be turned around. God's wrath,
like that of any good parent, is born out of love. It's hard to see

that in the moment, but it is true. Let's study just such a moment from the pages of the Bible.

Through Moses, God gave the Israelites these explicit instructions:

> *"'Do not make any gods to be alongside me; do not make for yourselves gods of silver or gods of gold....'"* (Exodus 20:23.)

And then we read the Israelites' response in Exodus 24:3:

> *When Moses went and told the people all the Lord's words and laws, they responded with one voice, "Everything the Lord has said we will do."*

But alas, we read these words in Exodus 32:1-10:

> *When the people saw that Moses was so long in coming down from the mountain, they gathered around Aaron and said, "Come, make us gods who will go before us. As for this fellow Moses who brought us up out of Egypt, we don't know what has happened to him."*
>
> *Aaron answered them, "Take off the gold earrings that your wives, your sons and your daughters are wearing, and bring them to me." So all the people took off their earrings and brought them to Aaron. He took what they handed him and made it into an idol cast in the shape of a calf, fashioning it with a tool. Then they said, "These are your gods, O Israel, who brought you up out of Egypt."*

When Aaron saw this, he built an altar in front of the calf and announced, "Tomorrow there will be a festival to the Lord." So the next day the people rose early and sacrificed burnt offerings and presented fellowship offerings. Afterward they sat down to eat and drink and got up to indulge in revelry.

Then the Lord said to Moses, "Go down, because your people, whom you brought up out of Egypt, have become corrupt. They have been quick to turn away from what I commanded them and have made themselves an idol cast in the shape of a calf. They have bowed down to it and sacrificed to it and have said, 'These are your gods, O Israel, who brought you up out of Egypt.'

"I have seen these people," the Lord said to Moses, "and they are a stiff-necked people. Now leave me alone so that my anger may burn against them and that I may destroy them. Then I will make you into a great nation."

That was certainly not an isolated incident of the Israelites' disobedience. Over and over, like a broken record, the people of Israel broke their connection with God and went their own way, which was downright disobedient. They did that in spite of their knowledge of what God expected and required of them. Certainly we must not become smug and shake our heads in amazement at their disobedience. It doesn't require much truthful soul searching to acknowledge the downright disobedience in our lives either. I don't think we realize just how much God hates, and I mean <u>hates</u>, His children's disobedience.

We do not like to relate words like hate, anger, and wrath with the Lord God. Whenever we do take the time to contemplate God's multiple attributes, we certainly tend to focus on the ones that bring us the most comfort. We receive comfort from God's love, mercy and grace. However, our thoughts of God's holiness, righteousness, and justice quickly move us out of our comfort zone. For then we have to face the reality that we cannot take our disobedience lightly. God certainly doesn't—it is very serious.

So why in the world would the Israelites "make" a god when they knew the one and only God and the command of God?

> *"'Do not make any gods to be alongside me; do not make for yourselves gods of silver or gods of gold....'"* (Exodus 20:23.)

After reading that very direct verse, it makes us wonder why the people of Israel still disobeyed God. But it is also a question we should ask ourselves, for we also know that command of God and can read chilling, convicting Scripture verses like this one from Isaiah:

> *"I am the Lord, and there is no other; apart from me there is no God. I will strengthen you, though you have not acknowledged me, so that from the rising of the sun to the place of its setting men may know there is none besides me. I am the Lord, and there is no other. I form the light and create darkness, I bring prosperity and create disaster; I, the Lord, do all these things"* (Isaiah 45:5-7).

So why do we put trust in our own type of "golden calf" (possessions, social status, wealth, power, etc.) when we claim to know the one and only sovereign God? I believe it is in part because we find it so much easier to believe in our earthly treasures—those things that we can see, touch, and control— rather than storing up our treasures in heaven and exercising our faith in God.

Certainly the Israelites were experiencing feelings of loss of control and being out of touch because Moses, who was their visible representative from God, had been on the mountain writing down God's law and had been away from them for quite some time. He was their spiritual leader. He tried to lead them in the ways of the Lord and keep them connected to God. They did not have access to the Scriptures the way we do today.

We can stay connected to God through prayer and reading His Word. This must be a daily discipline, because after only one day of being disconnected, God knows. After two days of being disconnected, we know. And after three days of being disconnected, everybody knows, because we fall back to our old ways and habits, and then "self" very slyly creeps back into control. Result? Our next misstep could lead to disaster. This is a dangerous world we live in. It is vitally important to stay in step with the Lord. Yes, we do have to live in this world—that is simple reality. But we do not have to live for this world—that is spiritual reality. We desperately need to walk closely with the Lord through the study of His Word and through prayer.

Prayer on behalf of the Israelites was Moses' response after God had told him of His plan to destroy them because of their disobedience and corruption.

But Moses sought the favor of the Lord his God. "O Lord," he said, "why should your anger burn against your people, whom you brought out

of Egypt with great power and a mighty hand?
Why should the Egyptians say, 'It was with evil
intent that he brought them out, to kill them in
the mountains and to wipe them off the face of
the earth'? Turn from your fierce anger; relent
and do not bring disaster on your people.
Remember your servants Abraham, Isaac and
Israel, to whom you swore by your own self: 'I
will make your descendants as numerous as the
stars in the sky and I will give your descendants
all this land I promised them, and it will be their
inheritance forever.'" Then the Lord relented
and did not bring on his people the disaster he
had threatened (Exodus 32:11-14).

Moses had sought the favor of the Lord for the Israelites
with that intercessory prayer, and the Lord relented. The
Israelites would not be destroyed. Moses' prayer and God's
will were a victorious match. We need to take a glance behind
this scene of God's apparent intent to relent and gather the
building blocks that were used in the construction of this
inspiring biblical illustration of praying for God's will. Let's
first look at what the Bible reveals to us about some of the
qualities of God's nature that relate to His answer to this
particular prayer.

"God is not a man, that he should lie, nor a son
of man, that he should change his mind"
(Numbers 23:19a).

"He who is the Glory of Israel does not lie or
change his mind; for he is not a man, that he
should change his mind" (1 Samuel 15:29).

With the light of truth from those verses illuminating our path, let's seek some insight and perspective about God's promises and prophesies. Let's consider Genesis 49:10,

> *"The scepter will not depart from Judah, nor the ruler's staff from between his feet, until he comes to whom it belongs and the obedience of the nations is his."*

This prophesy promised that Jesus, the Messiah, would be a descendant from the line of Judah. If the Lord had destroyed the Israelites and made Moses into a great nation, God's very explicit promise in Genesis 49:10 would not have come to pass because Moses was descended from the house of Levi (Exodus 2:1-10).

We can now see what God's plan was for the Israelites in Exodus 32, and Moses' intercessory prayer was in perfect harmony with the Lord's will.

> *"Does he speak and then not act? Does he promise and not fulfill?"* (Numbers 23:19b).

> *"Remember the former things, those of long ago; I am God, and there is no other; I am God, and there is none like me. I make known the end from the beginning, from ancient times, what is still to come. I say: My purpose will stand, and I will do all that I please"* (Isaiah 46:9-10).

Oh, don't you see the flow of grace coming from the very heart of God. From the promised Messiah prophesy to the relenting from the deserved destruction of the Israelites, God showers His children with His amazing grace. God had every right to destroy the Israelites (and we deserve the same fate) for disobedience, but yet He lavished His grace upon them as He also lavishes His grace upon us. His grace has no limits, it is measureless, and it abounds to all who name the name of Jesus as their Lord and Savior. That is astounding, unexplainable, and totally unconditional love.

Now, what does He want in return for that beautiful grace? YOU! He wants to direct your paths. He wants you to follow His ways. He wants to mold and make you after His will. He wants you to desire His will for your life even if it conflicts with your human desires.

God's will for us is to be conformed into the likeness of His Son, Jesus, who was the fulfillment of God's promised Messiah. Jesus obeyed His Father's will, and as difficult as that was, the honor of being the Savior for all mankind made it all worthwhile. He is exalted above every other name.

> *Therefore God exalted him to the highest place and gave him the name that is above every name, that at the name of Jesus every knee should bow, in heaven and on earth and under the earth, and every tongue confess that Jesus Christ is Lord, to the glory of God the Father* (Philippians 2:9-11).

The blessing He received for obedience to God's will was tremendous. God promises us bountiful blessings, too, when we obey Him and take on the likeness and character of Christ.

> *"Blessed are the poor in spirit, for theirs is the kingdom of heaven.*
> *Blessed are those who mourn, for they will be comforted.*

Blessed are the meek, for they will inherit the earth.

Blessed are those who hunger and thirst for righteousness, for they will be filled.

Blessed are the merciful, for they will be shown mercy.

Blessed are the pure in heart, for they will see God.

Blessed are the peacemakers, for they will be called sons of God.

Blessed are those who are persecuted because of righteousness, for theirs is the kingdom of heaven.

"Blessed are you when people insult you, persecute you and falsely say all kinds of evil against you because of me. Rejoice and be glad, because great is your reward in heaven, for in the same way they persecuted the prophets who were before you" (Matthew 5:3-12).

Blessed—an inner joy of spiritual well being that the world can't give or take away.

Poor in spirit—opposite of self-sufficient. It is total dependence on God.

Mourn—We are truly sorry for how our sins hurt the Lord and we seek His forgiveness when we confess our sins.

Meek—it is humility—seeing God in His place of authority and knowing our place beneath Him.

Hunger and thirst for righteousness—it is a deep and continuing desire to grow and mature in the Lord. It is completely satisfying.

Merciful—when we are willing to self-sacrifice for the needs of others.

Peacemakers—when we know God's peace personally and make peace with others.

Persecuted—when we are harassed, rejected, ridiculed, and maybe even martyred.

In other words, praying to become like Christ and obeying God the Father are worth it! We will never be sorry. There's no way our self-centered wills could ever match His blessing-filled will for us, believe it or not!

God loves to hear from our hearts, and we may express our hearts to Him through prayer. He understands our feelings, our hurts, our pain, and He knows all of our circumstances. He wants us to pour our hearts out to Him. Of course, He knows what we want. He knows everything. So cry it out. Let it out. Be honest. But then never fail to say and mean, "Your will be done" as you conclude your heartfelt prayer.

> *Instead, you ought to say, "If it is the Lord's will, we will live and do this or that"* (James 4:15).

That puts your life back into His loving, faithful, and competent hands. And once there, we would love to think that we would no longer be subject to panic attacks. However, even one of the most faithful kings of Judah suffered a severe panic attack when he doubted God's competency for dealing with his life.

2 Chronicles 29:1-2 gives us some background information on this faithful king—Hezekiah.

> *Hezekiah was twenty-five years old when he became king, and he reigned in Jerusalem twenty-nine years. His mother's name was Abijah, daughter of Zechariah. He did what*

*was right in the eyes of the Lord, just as his
father David had done.*

Hezekiah was a faithful and godly man. He loved the
Lord and was a very spiritual leader of the people of Israel. And
from the book of Isaiah, we are given the details that led to
Hezekiah's panic attack. When he was in his late 30's and still
without an heir, he became deathly ill. Let's pick up his story
from Scripture.

> *In those days Hezekiah became ill and
> was at the point of death. The prophet Isaiah son
> of Amoz went to him and said, "This is what the
> Lord says: Put your house in order, because you
> are going to die; you will not recover."*
>
> *Hezekiah turned his face to the wall and
> prayed to the Lord, "Remember, O Lord, how I
> have walked before you faithfully and with
> wholehearted devotion and have done what is
> good in your eyes. And Hezekiah wept bitterly*
> (Isaiah 38: 1–3).

When confronted with Isaiah's message, Hezekiah
poured out the anguish in his heart to the Lord in prayer. He
was devastated and could not understand why God would do
this after all that he had done for Him. Basically, Hezekiah
begged for his life rather than, by faith, surrendering his will to
God's will and believing with his heart that God knew what He
was doing even though Hezekiah hated the whole idea.

> *Then the word of the Lord came to Isaiah: "Go
> and tell Hezekiah, 'This is what the Lord, the
> God of your father David, says: I have heard
> your prayer and seen your tears; I will add*

fifteen years to your life. And I will deliver you and this city from the hand of the king of Assyria. I will defend this city'" (Isaiah 38:4-6).

Yes, God gave Hezekiah fifteen more years. But again, just as we looked behind the scene of God's will found in His answer to Moses' intercessory prayer in Exodus, we need to take a closer look here also. The first thing I want to address is that God was not impressed with King Hezekiah's claim that God owed him special consideration because Hezekiah did what was good in the Lord's eyes. That, sadly, triggered a memory for me of a story I shared in my first book, Have You Heard About That Fruit?

"On May 30, 1993, our oldest son Chad left for Marine Boot Camp in San Diego, California. For two years he had wanted to be a Marine. I thought we were all ready. In fact, I thought, 'Good, let the government teach him how to pick up his clothes, because somehow, I failed.'

"On the morning of the day he was going to leave, it sunk in. He was really leaving, and it would never be the same again. It hit me like a brick. Saying that goodbye was awful! I hurt so badly. That empty nest syndrome is for the birds, right moms?

"That night I tossed and turned. Peace was as far away as Chad was. I was still wide awake at 4:15 a.m. I remember looking at the clock, then sitting right up in bed and accusing the Lord of not being good on His Word. He promised peace in the midst of our storms, and what I was experiencing was a far cry from

peace. I even added, 'Lord, look at all I do for
You!' How pitiful. His concern is not with what
I do—but with who I am. In other words, when
He looks into my heart (the real me, motives and
all), what does He see? What <u>did</u> my poor heart
look like to Him at that moment? Certainly not
good."

I share that story with you so that you don't fall into that
trap yourself. For remember how easily we disconnect
ourselves from the Lord's leading. And it didn't take Hezekiah
long to disconnect from the Lord either. Hezekiah developed a
very self-absorbed and arrogant attitude. He also became very
uncaring, even toward the people he should have loved and
cared for the most (Isaiah 39). But don't you wonder how much
better it would have been for Hezekiah if, instead of his panic
attack, he would have been willing to say these beautiful,
trusting words, "Your will be done"?

Remember when we studied the Lord's purpose in
relenting to Moses' intercessory prayer? We discovered there
that if God had destroyed the Israelites and made Moses into a
great nation, God's prophesy about Jesus as the promised
Messiah descending from the line of Judah would not have
been possible, because Moses was descended from the house of
Levi. I believe we have a similar scenario here with Jesus as
our focal point again. For you see, God promised King David
that a descendent from his line would sit on David's throne to
perfectly fulfill the role of Redeemer for God's people—that
Redeemer is Jesus.

> *For to us a child is born, to us a son is given,*
> *and the government will be on his shoulders.*
> *And he will be called Wonderful Counselor,*
> *Mighty God, Everlasting Father, Prince of*

Peace. Of the increase of his government and peace there will be no end. He will reign on David's throne and over his kingdom, establishing and upholding it with justice and righteousness from that time on and forever. The zeal of the Lord Almighty will accomplish this (Isaiah 9:6-7).

Now let's review Matthew 1, which documents the genealogy of Jesus.

A record of the genealogy of Jesus Christ the son of David, the son of Abraham: (Matthew 1:1).

There are many names listed in Matthew 1:1-16, and I encourage you to not only read them, but also study the stories of the individuals listed there. But for our study on Hezekiah, let's zero in on David (v.6), Hezekiah (v.10), and Jesus (v.16). There is one critical name I skipped, but the Lord didn't. In verse 10, we find the name Manasseh, who was the son of Hezekiah. That's right, when Hezekiah was on his deathbed, he did not yet have an heir. However, when Hezekiah died and his son Manasseh became King, Manasseh was just twelve years old.

Manasseh was twelve years old when he became king, and he reigned in Jerusalem fifty-five years (2 Kings 21:1a).

This means that Manasseh, the heir required to continue the promised line of David that would lead to Jesus, was born during the fifteen years in question. God's will will be done.

His promises will be kept, and we have His Son as our Savior today.

And through faith in God's Son, I didn't lose heart when our son Jason disconnected from the Lord's leading for a few years. I begged the Lord in prayer daily to bring Jason back to Himself. I knew that was the Lord's will because He loves Jason even more than I do. Naturally, I did not want His timetable to take years. I wanted it to happen today, or at the latest, tomorrow. I learned that not only did I need to surrender my will and my Jason to the Lord, but also the timetable. God was working, and I had to wait.

During that waiting time, the Lord also molded me some more. He was doing so much more than what met the eye. He was changing hearts and lives. The Lord knew what Jason had to go through and just how long it would take, so that when Jason did realize what Jesus had done for him, his faith would be his—not mine, not his dad's, and not his brother's—but his. Jason is living proof that *old things* pass away and God makes *all things* new (2 Corinthians 5:17 KJV).

It still amazes me and brings tears to my eyes to hear Jason's life-changing testimony, to see his hard-surfaced character soften, and to watch him relate to struggling young people because he's "been there." A mother could not be more blessed. That's all I ever wanted for my boys—to know that they will spend their eternal life with Jesus, their Savior, in heaven. Yes, that is in their future, but because of Jesus, I also can know that they will have abundant life right now! When Jesus becomes our Savior, we see life through different eyes— eyes of the heart. The apostle Paul prays that those eyes are continuously being opened.

> *I keep asking that the God of our Lord Jesus Christ, the glorious Father, may give you the Spirit of wisdom and revelation, so that you may*

know him better. I pray also that the eyes of your heart may be enlightened in order that you may know the hope to which he has called you, the riches of his glorious inheritance in the saints, and his incomparably great power for us who believe. That power is like the working of his mighty strength, ...(Ephesians 1:17-19).

Slowly, but surely, the old nature decreases and the new nature takes over. I see that miraculously happening in me, and I see it happening in my boys. There's nothing that thrills me more.

Praise the Lord that He knows how <u>everything</u> is going to turn out, and that He's still in the miracle business of changing lives, getting us to finally surrender our will and pray for <u>His</u> good, pleasing, and perfect will.

LESSON 3

PRAYING FOR GOD'S WILL

1. Do you wonder if prayer changes anything? How can you know for sure?

2. What does God ask of you? (2 John 6a.)

3. Does God get mad? If yes, why? (Scripture proof, please.)

4. What are some of the gods you worship? Why do you do that?

5. What was God going to do to the Israelites and to Moses? What impact did Moses' prayer have, and why?

6. Describe God's grace. What does "blessed" mean?

7. Restate Matthew 5:3-12 in your own words.

8. How is prayer an expression of your heart to God?

9. What must you never forget to say when you pour out your heart to the Lord? Why is that a must? (James 4:15.)

10. What did Hezekiah pray for and what were the results?

11. What are the "eyes of your heart"?

12.   What is God's greatest miracle in your life?

4

THE
INTERCESSOR

Our study of Moses' intercessory prayer in Chapter 3 is just one example Scripture gives us to prove that prayer builds a solid, secure relationship between men (women) and God. It enables them as intercessors to go beyond themselves and watch God work through them and their circumstances on behalf of others. Whether it be patriarchs and prophets in the Old Testament or Jesus' disciples and apostles in the New Testament, if they were to have a tight and real relationship with God, they knew what it took—prayer.

Elijah prayed earnestly that it would not rain, and it did not for three and a half years. Then he prayed for rain and the heavens opened up.

> *Elijah was a man just like us. He prayed earnestly that it would not rain, and it did not rain on the land for three and a half years. Again he prayed, and the heavens gave rain, and the earth produced its crops* (James 5:17-18).

Prayer and praise enabled Paul and Silas to find joy even while they were in jail. During their captivity, they experienced such a violent earthquake that the foundations of the prison were shaken to the point that all the prison doors flew open and everyone's chains came loose. However, their foundation of faith in the Lord was not shaken. Despite being given the opportunity to escape, Paul and Silas chose to stay put as prisoners. As a result, they would be given the privilege of sharing their earthquake-proof foundation of faith with the jailer and his whole family, who all came to believe in God. What an inspirational story to illustrate how God can use us and our circumstances on behalf of others.

About midnight Paul and Silas were praying and singing hymns to God, and the other prisoners were listening to them. Suddenly there was such a violent earthquake that the foundations of the prison were shaken. At once all the prison doors flew open, and everybody's chains came loose. The jailer woke up, and when he saw the prison doors open, he drew his sword and was about to kill himself because he thought the prisoners had escaped. But Paul shouted, "Don't harm yourself! We are all here!"

The jailer called for lights, rushed in and fell trembling before Paul and Silas. He then brought them out and asked, "Sirs, what must I do to be saved?"

They replied, "Believe in the Lord Jesus, and you will be saved—you and your household." Then they spoke the word of the Lord to him and to all the others in his house. At that hour of the night the jailer took them and washed their wounds; then immediately he and all his family were baptized. The jailer brought them into his house and set a meal before them; he was filled with joy because he had come to believe in God—he and his whole family (Acts 16:25-34).

I am reminded of another Biblical earthquake experience. The after effects of that quake are still reverberating today, over two thousand years later.

And when Jesus had cried out again in a loud voice, he gave up his spirit. At that moment the curtain of the temple was torn in two from top to bottom. The earth shook and the rocks split. The tombs broke open and the bodies of many holy people who had died were raised to life. They came out of the tombs, and after Jesus' resurrection they went into the holy city and appeared to many people (Matthew 27:50-53).

Just as Jesus did for Silas and Paul's jailer and his family, He did for you and your family. For you see, faith-based prayer motivated Jesus to go to the cross so you and I could have eternal life.

After Jesus said this, he looked toward heaven and prayed: "Father, the time has come. Glorify your Son, that your Son may glorify you. For you granted him authority over all people that he might give eternal life to all those you have given him. Now this is eternal life: that they may know you, the only true God, and Jesus Christ, whom you have sent. I have brought you glory on earth by completing the work you gave me to do. And now, Father, glorify me in your presence with the glory I had with you before the world began" (John 17:1-5).

When a righteous man prays, watch out—it works.

The prayer of a righteous man is powerful and effective (James 5:16b).

Another righteous man whose belief in God's power is a wonderful example of faith that glorified God was Abraham. No, unlike Jesus, Abraham was not perfect, but his heart revealed a trusting relationship with his God that enabled him to put his one and only son on a sacrificial altar (Genesis 22:9-12). His faith is spoken of in the Hall of Faith.

> *By faith Abraham, when called to go to a place he would later receive as his inheritance, obeyed and went, even though he did not know where he was going. By faith he made his home in the promised land like a stranger in a foreign country; he lived in tents, as did Isaac and Jacob, who were heirs with him of the same promise. For he was looking forward to the city with foundations, whose architect and builder is God.*
>
> *By faith Abraham, even though he was past age—and Sarah herself was barren—was enabled to become a father because he considered him faithful who had made the promise. And so from this one man, and he as good as dead, came descendants as numerous as the stars in the sky and as countless as the sand on the seashore.*
>
> *All these people were still living by faith when they died. They did not receive the things promised; they only saw them and welcomed them from a distance. And they admitted that they were aliens and strangers on earth. People who say such things show that they are looking*

for a country of their own. If they had been thinking of the country they had left, they would have had opportunity to return. Instead, they were longing for a better country—a heavenly one. Therefore God is not ashamed to be called their God, for he has prepared a city for them.

By faith Abraham, when God tested him, offered Isaac as a sacrifice. He who had received the promises was about to sacrifice his one and only son, even though God had said to him, "It is through Isaac that your offspring will be reckoned." Abraham reasoned that God could raise the dead, and figuratively speaking, he did receive Isaac back from death (Hebrews 11:8-19).

Was not our ancestor Abraham considered righteous for what he did when he offered his son Isaac on the altar? You see that his faith and his actions were working together, and his faith was made complete by what he did. And the scripture was fulfilled that says, "Abraham believed God, and it was credited to him as righteousness," and he was called God's friend (James 2:21-23).

In addition to his Hall of Faith standing, Abraham is also a wonderful example for us to follow as an intercessory prayer warrior. When God called Abraham to begin his mission, Abraham brought along his nephew Lot. As they moved along toward the promised land, their flocks and herds became so great that the land could no longer support their combined herds. Abraham suggested that they separate, and he gave Lot the first pick. Lot looked over the landscape with his greedy human eyes only, not the eyes of his heart, and as a result he chose the land of Sodom and Gomorrah.

At first glance, those two cities appeared to be a good place to live, with land that was fertile and lush. But the inhabitants of those cities were wicked to the very core of their being. They were certainly not places where it would be desirable to absorb the abysmal culture thriving there while trying to properly raise a family.

It is very easy to pass judgment on Lot and feel that we would never have done what he did. But yet we cast our lot to the wind of chance regularly by making choices that appeal only to our desires of the flesh without giving consideration to the spiritual consequences. We get more concerned about what others think of us and what it looks like to them rather than what God thinks about us and how we look to Him, and our choices prove it. How easily we succumb to what this world defines as successful.

The overwhelming credit card debt says a lot about that, doesn't it? The world tells us our self-worth is based on what we have and then pressures us to over-extend ourselves beyond our means in order to get it. Just let me insert a little reminder here: self-worth is not based on anything this world has to offer us or what earthly treasurers we obtain (or charge!). Our worth in God's eyes is based solely on who we are because of Jesus Christ. That's an absolute—not open for debate or questions!

We live in a day and age where absolutes are falling by the wayside. I hear it said that there are exceptions to everything. However, when it comes to obedience, God demands it, and there is no room for discussion. This world has a "sucking" power. And if we are not cautious of that fact, we are caught in it before we even realize it, which is the exact trap the apostle Paul warned us of in Romans 12:2a,

*Do not conform any longer to the pattern of this
world, ...*

Feeling conspicuous or odd because of our actions is not
what we are comfortable with, but God wants—no, demands—
us to be set apart. Our lives should be oozing with love, joy,
peace, patience, kindness, goodness, faithfulness, gentleness,
and self-control. Those qualities are so unusual that when we do
exhibit them for others to see there is no doubt to Whom we
belong. Jesus said, in Matthew 7:20, that it is by those nine
outstanding qualities in our lives that others will recognize that
we belong to Him. Wearing the title or the label "Christian" sets
us apart from normal worldly expectations. It's unusual and
might even get others to call us a name or two.

One day a friend of mine introduced me to someone as a
[Christian] "fanatic." Later she called me to apologize, and I
told her I had considered it a compliment, not an insult. I told
her there was no need to apologize, because if that's the way I
appear, praise the Lord—I must not be blending into this
world's definition of right and wrong.

Accepting the culture of the day seems natural to us
because "everyone is doing it." But being culturally correct is
very seldom scripturally friendly. God's principles may seem
old fashioned to some, but God never changes. He's the same
yesterday, today, and forever, and He leaves no room for
compromise.

As we again focus on Lot's story, we certainly find him
having to make spiritual compromises in order to fit in at
Sodom and Gomorrah. Lot was operating his "vehicle of life"
with "self" at the controls, and disastrous consequences
occurred.

The longer Lot stayed in Sodom and Gomorrah, the
more he became like the wicked inhabitants of those cities. So
when the verdict came down that God was going to destroy

these horribly wicked cities, Abraham went to the Lord and pleaded with Him on Lot's behalf. Despite what Lot had become, Abraham loved his nephew and became his intercessor—the "go between." Lot was so blinded by sin that he didn't even feel the need to pray, so Abraham prayed in his place. The closer we are to individuals, the more it causes us to feel their joys and sorrows. What a privilege it is to be able to bring it all to the Lord on their behalf in prayer.

What an example that was of loving someone so much that even when Lot did not see his own sin, Abraham was willing to stand in for him and pray on his behalf. The greatest gift we can give to those we love is prayer. Do you love a special someone—friend or family member—enough to go to bat for him—intercede for him? That's grace—and it's gorgeous.

Let's read the entire story of how Abraham prayed for Lot.

> *Then the Lord said, "The outcry against Sodom and Gomorrah is so great and their sin so grievous that I will go down and see if what they have done is as bad as the outcry that has reached me. If not, I will know."*
>
> *The men turned away and went toward Sodom, but Abraham remained standing before the Lord. Then Abraham approached him and said: "Will you sweep away the righteous with the wicked? What if there are fifty righteous people in the city? Will you really sweep it away and not spare the place for the sake of the fifty righteous people in it? Far be it from you to do such a thing—to kill the righteous with the wicked, treating the righteous and the wicked*

alike. Far be it from you! Will not the Judge of all the earth do right?"

The Lord said, "If I find fifty righteous people in the city of Sodom, I will spare the whole place for their sake."

Then Abraham spoke up again: "Now that I have been so bold as to speak to the Lord, though I am nothing but dust and ashes, what if the number of the righteous is five less than fifty? Will you destroy the whole city because of five people?"

"If I find forty-five there," he said, "I will not destroy it."

Once again he spoke to him, "What if only forty are found there?"

He said, "For the sake of forty, I will not do it."

Then he said, "May the Lord not be angry, but let me speak. What if only thirty can be found there?"

He answered, "I will not do it if I find thirty there."

Abraham said, "Now that I have been so bold as to speak to the Lord, what if only twenty can be found there?"

He said, "For the sake of twenty, I will not destroy it."

Then he said, "May the Lord not be angry, but let me speak just once more. What if only ten can be found there?"

He answered, "For the sake of ten, I will not destroy it."

When the Lord had finished speaking with Abraham, he left, and Abraham returned home (Genesis 18:20-33).

From fifty, to forty-five, to forty, to thirty, to twenty, and finally to ten, God was patient with Abraham because He recognized that his persistence was driven by genuine love and concern for Lot and his family.

Appropriate persistence is a good thing. It proves just how sincere you really are and how much you really believe. Read the parable of Jesus on this very subject.

Then Jesus told his disciples a parable to show them that they should always pray and not give up. He said: "In a certain town there was a judge who neither feared God nor cared about men. And there was a widow in that town who kept coming to him with the plea, 'Grant me justice against my adversary.'

"For some time he refused. But finally he said to himself, 'Even though I don't fear God or care about men, yet because this widow keeps bothering me, I will see that she gets justice, so that she won't eventually wear me out with her coming!'"

And the Lord said, "Listen to what the unjust judge says. And will not God bring about justice for his chosen ones, who cry out to him day and night? Will he keep putting them off? I tell you, he will see that they get justice, and quickly. However, when the Son of Man comes, will he find faith on the earth?" (Luke 18:1-8).

Respectful, persistent prayer means that we really believe that what we are praying for is in God's will.

We can clearly see in Genesis 18:33 that the Lord was finished discussing this matter, and Abraham respected that and knew when to stop. The Lord will gladly hear the desires and pleas of our hearts, but there comes a time when we have to hand them all over to Him in faith, leave them there with Him, and trust His answers when they come.

God's answer was that Sodom and Gomorrah were to be destroyed. How sad that not even ten righteous people could be found in all the city of Sodom. What does that say about the spiritual condition of the human heart? God saw the hearts of the people of Sodom, and also of Lot and his family; He knew what He had to do.

What caused Lot and his family to stoop so low? What caused them to turn downright despicable? The answer is simple. They disconnected themselves from God and connected instead to the world. They let the world suck them into its appetizing but destructive mold.

The prayer lives of Abraham and Lot were completely different, and as a result their lives went in two different directions.

Two angels were sent from God to get Lot and his family out of the city. Lot's sons-in-law absolutely refused to go. Lot, his wife, and his two daughters had such tight ties to those evil cities that the angels had to literally grab their hands and drag them out. They were all warned not to look back. But Lot's wife needed one more fleeting glance, and because of her disobedience, God turned her into a pillar of salt.

But Lot's wife looked back, and she became a pillar of salt (Genesis 19:26).

The lives of Lot and his daughters were spared. But their story grew even more bleak. We read in Genesis 19 that Lot and his daughters were involved in incest. The two sons born to Lot's daughters from this sinful incestuous behavior were the ancestors of the Moabites and Ammonites. Those two nations were to become bitter enemies of Abraham's descendants—yes, the very same Abraham who was the intercessor with God on behalf of Lot and his family. What a vivid illustration of the insidious nature of sin as it relentlessly clings to us down through the ages.

Remember, regardless of the age we live in, it is not the condition of the physical location that creates cesspools like Sodom and Gomorrah. Rather, it is the condition of the sinful heart of man living in the physical location that makes it into an abomination to all that is holy.

We love to say that we have made incredible improvements in the quality of life in our day and age. And it is true that great strides have been made through technological and medical advancements. However, if you follow the news on a daily basis, if you can stomach it, it is painfully apparent that there has been no similar improvement in the sinful condition of man's heart.

Oh, but all is not lost. We are not without hope. The Answer follows us down through the ages. And through prayer, we can reach out and receive, through faith, the only Antidote for mankind's sinful nature.

> *Let us fix our eyes on Jesus, the author and perfecter of our faith, who for the joy set before him endured the cross, scorning its shame, and sat down at the right hand of the throne of God. Consider him who endured such opposition from sinful men, so that you will not grow weary and lose heart* (Hebrews 12:2-3).

In Romans 8:26-27 Paul reminds us of our intercessor who helps us in our weakness.

In the same way, the Spirit helps us in our weakness. We do not know what we ought to pray for, but the Spirit himself intercedes for us with groans that words cannot express. And he who searches our hearts knows the mind of the Spirit, because the Spirit intercedes for the saints in accordance with God's will (Romans 8:26-27).

When we pray and trust the Lord with all of our hearts, He in turn promises to make our ways clear. He directs our paths. Read Proverbs 3:5-6:

Trust in the Lord with all your heart,
And lean not on your own understanding;
In all your ways acknowledge Him,
And He shall direct your paths. (NKJV)

When our eyes stay fixed on Him, we discover that Jesus is our ultimate Intercessor. Consider just some of all that He did on our behalf.

- He left the glory of heaven and came to earth on our behalf when we needed Him most.
- He fulfilled God's Law perfectly on our behalf, for we were not capable.
- He was innocent, yet was beaten and crucified on our behalf when He carried the burden of our guilt to the cross.
- He suffered and died on our behalf to cleanse us from our sins.

- He defeated death and Satan on our behalf because He loves us.
- He returned to heaven on our behalf to prepare a place for us.
- He sent His Spirit on our behalf to be our counselor, teacher, friend, and prayer partner.

Once you come to know Jesus, you will trust Him. Once you trust Him, you will want to follow Him. I pray that before the clock strikes the Father's appointed hour for you to go, you choose Jesus to be the Intercessor for your eternal soul.

LESSON 4

THE INTERCESSOR

1. a. What kind of man was Abraham?
    b. What was his relationship to God?
    c. What identifies you as one who belongs to Jesus?

2. Who was Lot? Describe why he was in this serious predicament. What was the Lord going to do?

3. What was Lot's downfall?

4. What was Abraham's motive for praying for Lot?

5. What motivates you to pray for other people? Do you have anyone in your life right now for whom you should be praying?

6. God did not appear to be angry with Abraham's prayer persistence. How does this give us reassurance when we pray?

7. Why is respectful persistence a good thing?

8. How do you think Abraham knew how long to continue his pleading with God, and when to stop?

9. After you lay your request before the Lord, what must you do?

10.   What does Hebrews 12:2-3 mean to you?

11.   What is an intercessor? Do you have an intercessor? (Romans 8:26-27.)

12.   What does Proverbs 3:5-6 mean to you? What are the key words?

5

PRAYING FOR A SERVANT'S HEART

What God desires for us and what we desire for ourselves are more often than not world's apart—spiritual versus secular. Our natural human desires, unfortunately, fall right in line with the things the secular world programs us to believe should be near and dear to our hearts. How easily we are influenced, and even mesmerized, by the fame, power, and wealth of those the secular world bestows titles upon, such as "great," "glamorous," "star," and "hero."

With all that programming in place, is it any wonder we have a very difficult time embracing the totally opposite spiritual world philosophy taught by God, demonstrated by Jesus, and empowered by the Holy Spirit?

> *"When the Son of Man comes in his glory, and all the angels with him, he will sit on his throne in heavenly glory. All the nations will be gathered before him, and he will separate the people one from another as a shepherd separates the sheep from the goats. He will put the sheep on his right and the goats on his left.*
>
> *"Then the King will say to those on his right, 'Come, you who are blessed by my Father; take your inheritance, the kingdom prepared for you since the creation of the world. For I was hungry and you gave me something to eat, I was*

thirsty and you gave me something to drink, I was a stranger and you invited me in, I needed clothes and you clothed me, I was sick and you looked after me, I was in prison and you came to visit me.'

"Then the righteous will answer him, 'Lord, when did we see you hungry and feed you, or thirsty and give you something to drink? When did we see you a stranger and invite you in, or needing clothes and clothe you? When did we see you sick or in prison and go to visit you?'

"The King will reply, 'I tell you the truth, whatever you did for one of the least of these brothers of mine, you did for me.'

"Then he will say to those on his left, 'Depart from me, you who are cursed, into the eternal fire prepared for the devil and his angels. For I was hungry and you gave me nothing to eat, I was thirsty and you gave me nothing to drink, I was a stranger and you did not invite me in, I needed clothes and you did not cothe me, I was sick and in prison and you did not look after me.'

"They also will answer, 'Lord, when did we see you hungry or thirsty or a stranger or needing clothes or sick or in prison, and did not help you?'

"He will reply, 'I tell you the truth, whatever you did not do for one of the least of these, you did not do for me.'

"Then they will go away to eternal punishment, but the righteous to eternal life" (Matthew 25:31-46).

"...just as the Son of Man did not come to be served, but to serve, and to give his life as a ransom for many" (Matthew 20:28).

But now, by dying to what once bound us, we have been released from the law so that we serve in the new way of the Spirit, and not in the old way of the written code (Romans 7:6).

So how do we, while living in this world, change the direction of our deeply ingrained secular heart desires that glorify man to the spiritual heart desires that glorify God? We need to pray for a servant's heart. It's very clear from Scripture that the Lord doesn't want us to miss the joy of servanthood. Just read how He explains it to the mother of James and John in Matthew 20:20-23:

Then the mother of Zebedee's sons came to Jesus with her sons and, kneeling down, asked a favor of him.

"What is it you want?" he asked.

She said, "Grant that one of these two sons of mine may sit at your right and the other at your left in your kingdom."

"You don't know what you are asking," Jesus said to them. "Can you drink the cup I am going to drink?"

"We can," they answered.

Jesus said to them, "You will indeed drink from my cup, but to sit at my right or left is not for me to grant. These places belong to those for whom they have been prepared by my Father."

I'm sure she had a hard time figuring out what Jesus meant by those words. Moms want the best for their children, and most moms will do anything they can to see that they get it. James and John's mom thought she was doing the right thing trying to get her boys seated in the highest position right next to Jesus in His kingdom. She envisioned Jesus would be king on this earth and her sons would be in a notable position of fame, power, wealth, and authority. She would be so proud of them. They would be "somebody." So much trouble and anxiety are caused by everybody trying to be somebody. Even the other disciples of Jesus got all worked up about it when they heard that they could be pushed out of a better position. Jesus laid it all out and explained what a "somebody" really is in Matthew 20:24–28:

> *When the ten heard about this, they were indignant with the two brothers. Jesus called them together and said, "You know that the rulers of the Gentiles lord it over them, and their high officials exercise authority over them. Not so with you. Instead, whoever wants to become great among you must be your servant, and whoever wants to be first must be your slave— just as the Son of Man did not come to be served, but to serve, and to give his life as a ransom for many."*

We couldn't have a greater example of a servant's heart than the heart of Jesus. If you want a pattern for what it really means to be "somebody"—look to Jesus. He is the pinnacle, the ultimate, a <u>real</u> hero. He was willing to become a servant for us, and, in turn, raised believers to the level of children of Almighty God. Doesn't that put all of this world's defined "somebodies" in a different light? Following Jesus' example, we find that we serve not because we aren't important, but in truth, because we are.

His servanthood was of the highest spiritual calling, but in the mind's eyes of this world, He was brought down to the lowest secular calling.

> *He was despised and rejected by men, a man of sorrows, and familiar with suffering.*
>
> *Like one from whom men hide their faces he was despised, and we esteemed him not.*
>
> *Surely he took up our infirmities and carried our sorrows, yet we considered him stricken by God, smitten by him, and afflicted.*
>
> *But he was pierced for our transgressions, he was crushed for our iniquities; the punishment that brought us peace was upon him, and by his wounds we are healed.*
>
> *We all, like sheep, have gone astray, each of us has turned to his own way; and the Lord has laid on him the iniquity of us all.*
>
> *He was oppressed and afflicted, yet he did not open his mouth; he was led like a lamb to the slaughter, and as a sheep before her shearers is silent, so he did not open his mouth.*
>
> *By oppression and judgment he was taken away. And who can speak of his descendants?*
>
> *For he was cut off from the land of the living; for the transgression of my people he was stricken.*
>
> *He was assigned a grave with the wicked, and with the rich in his death, though he had done no violence, nor was any deceit in his mouth* (Isaiah 53:3-9).

He was totally innocent and falsely accused. Yet Jesus chose not to open His mouth in His defense, and He did that as only an obedient servant would do to honor the Father. For over and over we read those Isaiah passages quoted in the New Testament as God's prophesy being fulfilled by the actions of Jesus. And, in turn, the Father blessed Him with the satisfaction and joy of completing His mission of servanthood on behalf of all the world. That was self-sacrifice. It was love at its greatest.

How do we change our minds and our attitudes about servanthood? For example, while I've been on my hands and knees cleaning my floor (I still like doing it the old fashioned way), or shoveling dirt for a landscaping project, I'll admit I've said to myself, "I'm sure (so and so) doesn't have to work like this; he or she just 'calls' someone." It all sounds so well and good to dream about delegating to someone else all the things we really don't like or want to do. However, if I had done that, I would have missed the blessing and satisfaction of completing the project and enjoying the results of service and a job well done.

How can we look at service as a privilege rather than a duty? The answer is simple—PRAYER. We have to connect with our God, and He can help us see others through the eyes of Jesus, use us with the very attitude of Jesus, and equip us with everything we need so that the work is done to give glory to the Father. Oh, how Jesus loves for the Father to receive glory.

Let us be reminded again from Isaiah 42:5, 8-9, who our God is and just how capable He is:

> *This is what God the Lord says—he who created the heavens and stretched them out, who spread out the earth and all that comes out of it, who gives breath to its people, and life to those who walk on it:* (v.5).

> *"I am the Lord; that is my name! I will not give my glory to another or my praise to idols.*
>
> *See, the former things have taken place, and new things I declare; before they spring into being I announce them to you"* (v. 8-9).

As God enabled Jesus to serve:

> *"Here is my servant, whom I uphold, my chosen one in whom I delight; I will put my Spirit on him and he will bring justice to the nations"* (Isaiah 42:1).

He is more than capable to enable us when He calls us to serve:

> *"But when he, the Spirit of truth, comes, he will guide you into all truth. He will not speak on his own; he will speak only what he hears, and he will tell you what is yet to come. He will bring glory to me by taking from what is mine and making it known to you. All that belongs to the Father is mine. That is why I said the Spirit will take from what is mine and make it known to you"* (John 16:13-15).

> *"...the Father himself loves you because you have loved me and have believed that I came from God"* (John 16:27).

We have all that we need and all that it takes to do what God has called us to do. What a wonderful, loving, and empowering truth that is. He never expected us to do His service without divine support. He knew we never could, so now Jesus puts His Spirit in us to fill our minds and hearts with Himself, affecting everything about us.

So often when we think of working for God, letting Him use us, or fulfilling the mission He's called us to do, we tend to think of the foreign field—an assignment in the jungle, the Congo, or way out in the bush somewhere. And sometimes it does mean that. But when God calls people for those missions, He gives them a burning desire and a love to be there.

When I was younger, I was so afraid to surrender my life to the Lord because I was sure He would send me to Africa, and I didn't want to go there. But a friend of mine did get just such a calling from the Lord to be a missionary in Africa, and she would not have it any other way.

Being a servant of the Lord Jesus doesn't always require us to move away. One of the greatest mission assignments can be right where we live. He calls each of us to a certain spouse or roommate, a child, a place in a church or on a committee, a neighborhood, or a workplace. The list could go on and on. If we truly desire that title of "servant of the Lord Jesus," the Lord will put us in the right place at the right time and give us what it takes to do the "job."

The Lord did not call me to go to Africa because He had ordained a different mission for me (Psalm 139:16). He's ordained a specific mission for you, too; and believe it or not, your life will not be completely satisfying until you accept that mission for Him and allow Him to do what He wants to do through you to accomplish it. Always remember, every mission is of equal importance to Him.

> *...your eyes saw my unformed body. All the days ordained for me were written in your book before one of them came to be* (Psalm 139:16).

My very close friend, Bonni, was ordained by God to be the mother of a special needs child. Bonni was "chosen" to pray through surgery after surgery for her son, experience the stares her son received from strangers, and answer her child's question, "Why does God make handicapped children, anyway?" And through it all, she fights her own exhaustion from this (I'm sure it sometimes seems to her) never ending situation. How easy it would be for her to scream with self-pity—and she would be the first to say that there are days..., but then she prays and stays connected with her God, who promises to be wings under which she can take refuge—her strength, her fortress, and her God in whom she can put her trust (see Psalms 17, 18, and 91).

She has learned that she can lean on His promises, and they are more than sufficient in His calling and purpose for her. As a result, she finds peace, rest, and satisfaction in her mission. For her, there is no higher calling—no greater privilege. And may I say, she is one fabulous mother and one powerful tool used of the Lord to impact many with her servant's heart. Her mission is personal, right there where she lives, but by her example she is reaching out and touching others put in her path by God Himself. It only takes one little spark to start a huge fire. Do not underestimate what God can do through you and your mission assignment, and please,

Let us not become weary in doing good, for at the proper time we will reap a harvest if we do not give up (Galatians 6:9).

I use the passage again from Isaiah 6 to let Isaiah share with us what happened to him during one of his prayer times. At that particular time, God had revealed His mission for Isaiah. God knew exactly how to do it, too.

*In the year that King Uzziah died, I saw
the Lord seated on a throne, high and exalted,
and the train of his robe filled the temple. Above
him were seraphs, each with six wings: With two
wings they covered their faces, with two they
covered their feet, and with two they were flying.
And they were calling to one another:*

*"Holy, holy, holy is the Lord Almighty;
the whole earth is full of his glory."*

*At the sound of their voices the doorposts
and thresholds shook and the temple was filled
with smoke* (Isaiah 6:1-4).

What a visual! The Lord, on the throne, high and
exalted, the angels proclaiming His holiness and glory, and His
power so great it shook the room and filled it with smoke.

What was the impact on Isaiah? He saw the Lord in His
mighty place and could not help but see himself in his place.

*"Woe to me!" I cried. "I am ruined! For I am a
man of unclean lips, and I live among a people
of unclean lips, and my eyes have seen the King,
the Lord Almighty"* (Isaiah 6:5).

The Lord did not leave Isaiah (nor will He ever leave us,
for that matter) in that hopeless state.

*Then one of the seraphs flew to me with a live
coal in his hand, which he had taken with tongs
from the altar. With it he touched my mouth and
said, "See, this has touched your lips; your guilt
is taken away and your sin atoned for"*
(Isaiah 6:6-7).

Jesus is our live coal, the ultimate servant sacrifice that touches our being with His blood and takes away our sin and guilt. After studying this in one of the Bible studies I lead, we decided that our group should be known as "The Fellowship of Burnt Lips." We are women touched, cleansed, and saved by grace. What a redeeming picture!

Isaiah also listened during his prayer time (reminder—don't forget to listen during your prayer time!) and heard the Lord ask this question:

> *Then I heard the voice of the Lord saying,*
> *"Whom shall I send? And who will go for us?"*
> (Isaiah 6:8a).

Because of the beautiful vision he had just witnessed, his immediate response was,

> *And I said, "Here am I. Send me!"* (Isaiah 6:8b).

Did you notice that the Lord did not force him, pin him down, or make him feel obligated? The Lord did not have to. He knew that if Isaiah got a glimpse of what was done for him, Isaiah would respond, *"Here am I. Send me!"* Each one of us who has been saved by the Servant should be saying without hesitation, *"Here am I. Send me!"*

The Lord is very clear, as that chapter in Isaiah continues, that the mission will not always be easy or fall on receptive ears. Many will not understand or agree. Some will choose to close their eyes, ears, and hearts to their need for a Savior. Some may develop a spiritual dullness. Others may fear that when the "light" is directed on them, it will expose them in a way they do not want to be seen by others (or even by themselves). They are not going to take too kindly to that, and we might become their punching bag.

Isaiah naturally asks this question in verse 11 after wholeheartedly accepting the mission in verse 8.

> *Then I said, "For how long, O Lord?"*
> *And he answered:*
> *"Until the cities lie ruined and without inhabitant, until the houses are left deserted and the fields ruined and ravaged,..."*(Isaiah 6:11).

That is a long-term mission assignment! The Lord responds by encouraging Isaiah, and us as well, to tell the story, to live out our personal salvation story over and over for as long as it takes. Do not give up! Do not be discouraged! How people respond to our witness is their choice, but they need to hear and see the gospel story, and that is our choice.

There is no doubt about it—servanthood has a high price tag. But the reward outweighs it all. What is our reward? Jesus has been exalted to the name above all names, and He will welcome us to a place in His kingdom, worshiping at Jehovah's feet, singing the "Hallelujah Chorus" and "Amazing Grace" in our Savior's presence, where there will be no more sickness, pain, tears, or goodbyes—a place where there will be peace forever. Yes, it is worth it all!

One last thought on this subject. Whenever you feel like you are being taken for granted, or there is no appreciation for your servant's heart, stop and ask yourself, "Am I working to hear appreciation and approval from mankind in this world, or, *'Well done, good and faithful servant!'* (Matthew 25:23) from Almighty God when I get to heaven?" Is the mission assignment He's asked of you a privilege or a duty? Only you can answer that question, but before you answer, think of all He's done for you.

The title of "servant of the Lord Jesus" is more honoring and fulfilling than any earthly title this world can bestow upon us. Pray for a heart like the heart of Jesus—a servant's heart!

LESSON 5

PRAYING FOR A SERVANT'S HEART

1. Read Matthew 20:20-28. What is the world's definition of greatness? What is Jesus' definition of greatness?

2. Read Isaiah 53:3-9. Jesus was our greatest example of servanthood. What was Jesus willing to look like and be treated like for you and me?

3. What is the difference between privilege and duty?

4. How and why does prayer change your attitude toward servanthood?

5. From Isaiah 42:5-9, describe who God is and what He has done.

6. When God calls, He equips. How did He equip Jesus? (Isaiah 42:1.) How does He equip us? (John 16:13-15, 27.)

7. What is your personal mission that He has ordained for you?

8. In Isaiah's prayer time, what did he see? (Isaiah 6.) What did he hear? What did he literally feel? What do you think was going through his mind during this magnificent experience?

9.   How did Isaiah see himself?

10.   Describe what the angel did for Isaiah and how that relates to you.

11.   What did the Lord ask, and what was Isaiah's response? Have you ever said those words? Should you? Why?

12.   What will be your reward for serving the Lord?

6

PRAYING
THE SCRIPTURES

In this chapter, you will not be reading many of my words, but rather His words. There are times in our lives when human words, no matter how true or sincere, just do not have the strength or fortitude to get us through. That is when His Word lifts us up and carries us.

Have you ever found yourself in the middle of difficult circumstances and wondered, "Where can I go for help?" As always, the answer is, "To the Lord." There is no one better.

And the beautiful reality is that you don't have far to go because the Lord is right there in the middle of your circumstances, waiting for you to reach out (remember, prayer is the "heart changer and mountain mover") and find that He is all-sufficient. From the book of Isaiah, we can read this verse and know He's sufficient and competent.

> *For to us a child is born, to us a son is given, and the government will be on his shoulders.*
>
> *And he will be called Wonderful Counselor, Mighty God, Everlasting Father, Prince of Peace* (Isaiah 9:6).

His names alone prove it all. Those inspiring names of our Lord leave no room for doubt as to whom we should be seeking, for He is the:

Wonderful Counselor—He knows His course of action for our lives and knows how to carry it out. And when praying from His Word, we find that He is the best advice giver. Jesus said that our Father in heaven knows what we need even before we ask Him (Matthew 6:8).

Mighty God—He has divine power. No human power can compare.

Everlasting Father—He will endure. He is a compassionate and loving provider.

Prince of Peace—He brings peace into the heart of every believer; and upon His triumphant return, His rule will bring a unity among individuals as well as the whole universe.

Our greatest resource for what to pray comes from the truth of Scripture revealed to us through the empowering understanding of the Holy Spirit. Praying Scripture not only connects us with God, but through His Word we also hear Him speak to us. If we do not direct our minds to Scripture, our human feelings will ride right over our faith. We cannot deny our feelings. They are a big part of us. However, they must stay in check. They must never get to the point that they overpower us. And that can happen easily, because our feelings are so automatic and natural, especially when the circumstances affect someone very close—someone we love more than life itself. For example, a child.

Our son Chad, who is a church pastor, is very physically fit and works hard to keep it that way. (I guess it's still the Marine in him.) A year ahead of time, he asked his dad and me if we would like to go along with him, his wife, and our precious granddaughter to the gorgeous village of Lake Placid in New York. Of course, we were thrilled to go on a beautiful vacation with them. Then he went on to tell us why we would be going to that particular place at that particular time. He was going to be a participant in the Ironman Triathlon—a 2.4 mile swim, 112-mile bike ride, and then a 26-mile marathon. My first thought was, "Why would he want to put himself through that?" but I could tell it meant a lot to him, so I kept that thought to myself.

It is an understatement to say that taking the trip together and watching Chad compete in the triathlon was an exciting adventure. But little did I expect the emotional roller coaster ride I experienced supporting Chad as he participated in the triathlon. I experienced my emotions going from anticipation and excitement, to anxiousness and fear, to agony and discouragement, and finally to joy and exhilaration. After completing the swim and an excruciating bike ride up the hills of the Adirondacks in 25 – 30 mile per hour winds and pouring rain, he was in the third segment of the race (the marathon) when he passed us along the route and told us he didn't think he could finish the race. His face said all that was needed for me to want to take matters into my own hands; and even though he's bigger than I am, I wanted to go right out there and put him on my back and carry him the rest of the way to the finish line.

Praying Scripture was all that I had to hang onto, and I reached out and used it in every way I knew how. I believe to this day that it was faith-based prayer that brought him in. As he ran into the arena with thousands of people screaming (especially the four of us), I saw the look of victory and accomplishment on his face as he crossed the finish line. He did it! It was one of the most emotional days of my life. I do believe I felt most of the broad range of human emotions anyone could have in just that one day.

How can we prevent our feelings from overpowering us or our doubts from confusing us? Pray Scripture. It never fails! Please take the time to read these verses. The Lord wants to meet us at our point of need.

When we are consumed with anxiety—

> *"Even to your old age and gray hairs I am he, I am he who will sustain you. I have made you and I will carry you; I will sustain you and I will rescue you"* (Isaiah 46:4).

> *"For I know the plans I have for you,"* declares the Lord, *"plans to prosper you and not to harm you, plans to give you hope and a future. Then you will call upon me and come and pray to me, and I will listen to you. You will seek me and find me when you seek me with all your heart"* (Jeremiah 29:11-13).

> *Humble yourselves, therefore, under God's mighty hand, that he may lift you up in due time. Cast all your anxiety on him because he cares for you* (1 Peter 5:6-7).

When we are overcome with fear—

> *"So do not fear, for I am with you; do not be dismayed, for I am your God. I will strengthen you and help you; I will uphold you with my righteous right hand"* (Isaiah 41:10).

> *"So do not be afraid of them. There is nothing concealed that will not be disclosed, or hidden that will not be made known. What I tell you in the dark, speak in the daylight; what is whispered in your ear, proclaim from the roofs. Do not be afraid of those who kill the body but cannot kill the soul. Rather, be afraid of the One*

*who can destroy both soul and body in hell. Are
not two sparrows sold for a penny? Yet not one
of them will fall to the ground apart from the will
of your Father. And even the very hairs of your
head are all numbered. So don't be afraid; you
are worth more than many sparrows"*
(Matthew 10:26-31).

When we are overwrought with worry—

*"Therefore I tell you, do not worry about
your life, what you will eat or drink; or about
your body, what you will wear. Is not life more
important than food, and the body more
important than clothes? Look at the birds of the
air; they do not sow or reap or store away in
barns, and yet your heavenly Father feeds them.
Are you not much more valuable than they? Who
of you by worrying can add a single hour to his
life?*

*"And why do you worry about clothes?
See how the lilies of the field grow. They do not
labor or spin. Yet I tell you that not even
Solomon in all his splendor was dressed like one
of these. If that is how God clothes the grass of
the field, which is here today and tomorrow is
thrown into the fire, will he not much more
clothe you, O you of little faith? So do not worry,
saying, 'What shall we eat?' or 'What shall we
drink?' or 'What shall we wear?' For the
pagans run after all these things, and your
heavenly Father knows that you need them. But
seek first his kingdom and his righteousness, and
all these things will be given to you as well.*

Therefore do not worry about tomorrow, for tomorrow will worry about itself. Each day has enough trouble of its own" (Matthew 6:25-34).

When we are emotionally tired—

"Come to me, all you who are weary and burdened, and I will give you rest. Take my yoke upon you and learn from me, for I am gentle and humble in heart, and you will find rest for your souls. For my yoke is easy and my burden is light" (Matthew 11:28-30).

Therefore, my dear brothers, stand firm. Let nothing move you. Always give yourselves fully to the work of the Lord, because you know that your labor in the Lord is not in vain (1 Corinthians 15:58).

Let us not become weary in doing good, for at the proper time we will reap a harvest if we do not give up. Therefore, as we have opportunity, let us do good to all people, especially to those who belong to the family of believers (Galatians 6:9-10).

When we are feeling weak—

Wait for the Lord; be strong and take heart and wait for the Lord (Psalm 27:14).

...in all these things we are more than conquerors through him who loved us (Romans 8:37).

When we are consumed with anger, bitterness, or a critical spirit—

> *But you, O Lord, are a compassionate and gracious God, slow to anger, abounding in love and faithfulness* (Psalm 86:15).

> *A fool gives full vent to his anger, but a wise man keeps himself under control* (Proverbs 29:11).

> *Love is patient, love is kind. It does not envy, it does not boast, it is not proud. It is not rude, it is not self-seeking, it is not easily angered, it keeps no record of wrongs. Love does not delight in evil but rejoices with the truth. It always protects, always trusts, always hopes, always perseveres* (1 Corinthians 13:4-7).

> *"In your anger do not sin": Do not let the sun go down while you are still angry, and do not give the devil a foothold* (Ephesians 4:26-27).

> *My dear brothers, take note of this: Everyone should be quick to listen, slow to speak and slow to become angry, for man's anger does not bring about the righteous life that God desires* (James 1:19-20).

When we are filled with discouragement—

> *Cast your cares on the Lord and he will sustain you; he will never let the righteous fall* (Psalm 55:22).

But we have this treasure in jars of clay to show that this all-surpassing power is from God and not from us. We are hard pressed on every side, but not crushed; perplexed, but not in despair; persecuted, but not abandoned; struck down, but not destroyed. We always carry around in our body the death of Jesus, so that the life of Jesus may also be revealed in our body. For we who are alive are always being given over to death for Jesus' sake, so that his life may be revealed in our mortal body. So then, death is at work in us, but life is at work in you.

It is written: "I believed; therefore I have spoken." With that same spirit of faith we also believe and therefore speak, because we know that the one who raised the Lord Jesus from the dead will also raise us with Jesus and present us with you in his presence. All this is for your benefit, so that the grace that is reaching more and more people may cause thanksgiving to overflow to the glory of God.

Therefore we do not lose heart. Though outwardly we are wasting away, yet inwardly we are being renewed day by day. For our light and momentary troubles are achieving for us an eternal glory that far outweighs them all. So we fix our eyes not on what is seen, but on what is unseen. For what is seen is temporary, but what is unseen is eternal (2 Corinthians 4:7-18).

When we are looking straight into the face of a crisis—

I lift up my eyes to the hills—where does my help come from?

My help comes from the Lord, the Maker of heaven and earth.

He will not let your foot slip—he who watches over you will not slumber; indeed, he who watches over Israel will neither slumber nor sleep.

The Lord watches over you—the Lord is your shade at your right hand; the sun will not harm you by day, nor the moon by night.

The Lord will keep you from all harm— he will watch over your life; the Lord will watch over your coming and going both now and forevermore (Psalm 121).

When we feel beat up—

What, then, shall we say in response to this? If God is for us, who can be against us? He who did not spare his own Son, but gave him up for us all—how will he not also, along with him, graciously give us all things? Who will bring any charge against those whom God has chosen? It is God who justifies. Who is he that condemns? Christ Jesus, who died—more than that, who was raised to life—is at the right hand of God and is also interceding for us. Who shall separate us from the love of Christ? Shall trouble or hardship or persecution or famine or nakedness or danger or sword? As it is written:

"For your sake we face death all day long; we are considered as sheep to be slaughtered."

No, in all these things we are more than conquerors through him who loved us. For I am convinced that neither death nor life, neither angels nor demons, nether the present nor the future, nor any powers, neither height nor depth, nor anything else in all creation, will be able to separate us from the love of God that is in Christ Jesus our Lord (Romans 8:31-39).

We write this to make our joy complete.

This is the message we have heard from him and declare to you: God is light; in him there is no darkness at all. If we claim to have fellowship with him yet walk in darkness, we lie and do not live by the truth. But if we walk in the light, as he is in the light, we have fellowship with one another, and the blood of Jesus, his Son, purifies us from all sin.

If we claim to be without sin, we deceive ourselves and the truth is not in us. If we confess our sins, he is faithful and just and will forgive us our sins and purify us from all unrighteousness (1 John 1:4-9).

When it seems impossible to face tomorrow—

God is our refuge and strength, an ever-present help in trouble (Psalm 46:1).

"Be still, and know that I am God; I will be exalted among the nations, I will be exalted in the earth." (Psalm 46:10).

He who dwells in the shelter of the Most High will rest in the shadow of the Almighty.

I will say of the Lord, "He is my refuge and my fortress, my God, in whom I trust."

Surely he will save you from the fowler's snare and from the deadly pestilence.
He will cover you with his feathers, and under his wings you will find refuge; his faithfulness will be your shield and rampart (Psalm 91:1-4).

"Because he loves me," says the Lord, "I will rescue him; I will protect him, for he acknowledges my name. He will call upon me, and I will answer him; I will be with him in trouble, I will deliver him and honor him." (Psalm 91:14-15).

In my anguish I cried to the Lord, and he answered by setting me free. The Lord is with me; I will not be afraid. What can man do to me? The Lord is with me; he is my helper. I will look in triumph on my enemies (Psalm 118:5-7).

One day Jesus said to his disciples, "Let's go over to the other side of the lake." So they got into a boat and set out. As they sailed, he fell asleep. A squall came down on the lake, so that the boat was being swamped, and they were in great danger.
The disciples went and woke him, saying, "Master, Master, we're going to drown!"
He got up and rebuked the wind and the raging waters; the storm subsided, and all was calm. "Where is your faith?" he asked his disciples.
In fear and amazement they asked one another, "Who is this? He commands even the

winds and the water, and they obey him"
(Luke 8:22-25).

When we feel so all alone—

*The Lord is my shepherd, I shall not be in
want. He makes me lie down in green pastures,
he leads me beside quiet waters, he restores my
soul. He guides me in paths of righteousness for
his name's sake. Even though I walk through the
valley of the shadow of death, I will fear no evil,
for you are with me; your rod and your staff,
they comfort me.*
*You prepare a table before me in the
presence of my enemies. You anoint my head
with oil; my cup overflows. Surely goodness and
love will follow me all the days of my life, and I
will dwell in the house of the Lord forever*
(Psalm 23).

"Never will I leave you; never will I forsake you"
(Hebrews 13:5b).

When we need to know which way to go or what decision to make—

*I will instruct you and teach you in the way you
should go; I will counsel you and watch over you*
(Psalm 32:8).

*Trust in the Lord with all your heart and lean not
on your own understanding; in all your ways
acknowledge him, and he will make your paths
straight* (Proverbs 3:5-6).

This is what the Lord says—your Redeemer, the Holy One of Israel: "I am the Lord your God, who teaches you what is best for you, who directs you in the way you should go (Isaiah 48:17).

When we are overcome with sorrow—

"Blessed are those who mourn, for they will be comforted" (Matthew 5:4).

"Do not let your hearts be troubled. Trust in God; trust also in me. In my Father's house are many rooms; if it were not so, I would have told you. I am going there to prepare a place for you. And if I go and prepare a place for you, I will come back and take you to be with me that you also may be where I am. You know the way to the place where I am going" (John 14:1-4).

I consider that our present sufferings are not worth comparing with the glory that will be revealed in us (Romans 8:18).

And we know that in all things God works for the good of those who love him, who have been called according to his purpose (Romans 8:28).

Praise be to the God and Father of our Lord Jesus Christ, the Father of compassion and the God of all comfort, who comforts us in all our troubles, so that we can comfort those in any trouble with the comfort we ourselves have received from God (2 Corinthians 1:3-4).

Brothers, we do not want you to be ignorant about those who fall asleep, or to grieve like the rest of men, who have no hope. We believe that Jesus died and rose again and so we believe that God will bring with Jesus those who have fallen asleep in him. According to the Lord's own word, we tell you that we who are still alive, who are left till the coming of the Lord, will certainly not precede those who have fallen asleep. For the Lord himself will come down from heaven, with a loud command, with the voice of the archangel and with the trumpet call of God, and the dead in Christ will rise first. After that, we who are still alive and are left will be caught up together with them in the clouds to meet the Lord in the air. And so we will be with the Lord forever. Therefore encourage each other with these words (1 Thessalonians 4:13-18).

When we hurt so badly—

Going a little farther, he fell with his face to the ground and prayed, "My Father, if it is possible, may this cup be taken from me. Yet not as I will, but as you will" (Matthew 26:39).

Not only so, but we also rejoice in our sufferings, because we know that suffering produces perseverance; perseverance, character; and character, hope. And hope does not disappoint us, because God has poured out his love into our hearts by the Holy Spirit, whom he has given us (Romans 5:3-5).

But he said to me, "My grace is sufficient for you, for my power is made perfect in weakness." Therefore I will boast all the more gladly about my weaknesses, so that Christ's power may rest on me. That is why, for Christ's sake, I delight in weaknesses, in insults, in hardships, in persecutions, in difficulties. For when I am weak, then I am strong (2 Corinthians 12:9-10).

Dear friends, do not be surprised at the painful trial you are suffering, as though something strange were happening to you. But rejoice that you participate in the sufferings of Christ, so that you may be overjoyed when his glory is revealed (1 Peter 4:12-13).

So then, those who suffer according to God's will should commit themselves to their faithful Creator and continue to do good (1 Peter 4:19).

How we turn our panic into peace—

You will keep in perfect peace him whose mind is steadfast, because he trusts in you. Trust in the Lord forever, for the Lord, the Lord, is the Rock eternal (Isaiah 26:3-4).

"I have told you these things, so that in me you may have peace. In this world you will have trouble. But take heart! I have overcome the world" (John 16:33).

For he himself is our peace, who has made the two one and has destroyed the barrier, the dividing wall of hostility, ... " (Ephesians 2:14).

Do not be anxious about anything, but in everything, by prayer and petition, with thanksgiving, present your requests to God. And the peace of God, which transcends all understanding, will guard your hearts and your minds in Christ Jesus (Philippians 4:6-7).

When we feel we cannot fight temptation—

Search me, O God, and know my heart; test me and know my anxious thoughts. See if there is any offensive way in me, and lead me in the way everlasting (Psalm 139:23-24).

"Watch and pray so that you will not fall into temptation. The spirit is willing, but the body is weak" (Matthew 26:41).

So, if you think you are standing firm, be careful that you don't fall! No temptation has seized you except what is common to man. And God is faithful; he will not let you be tempted beyond what you can bear. But when you are tempted, he will also provide a way out so that you can stand up under it.
Therefore, my dear friends, flee from idolatry (1 Corinthians 10:12-14).

Finally, brothers, whatever is true, whatever is noble, whatever is right, whatever is pure, whatever is lovely, whatever is admirable—if anything is excellent or praiseworthy—think about such things (Philippians 4:8).

Submit yourselves, then, to God. Resist the devil, and he will flee from you (James 4:7).

Therefore, dear friends, since you already know this, be on your guard so that you may not be carried away by the error of lawless men and fall from your secure position (2 Peter 3:17).

When we begin to doubt—

Those who trust in the Lord are like Mount Zion, which cannot be shaken but endures forever (Psalm 125:1).

"...in quietness and trust is your strength,..." (Isaiah 30:15b).

Jesus replied, "I tell you the truth, if you have faith and do not doubt, not only can you do what was done to the fig tree, but also you can say to this mountain, 'Go, throw yourself into the sea,' and it will be done. If you believe, you will receive whatever you ask for in prayer" (Matthew 21:21-22).

When we are connected to God in prayer, we want what He wants. We then receive what we ask for because it is in accordance with His perfect will. We then begin to understand and accept—

"For my thoughts are not your thoughts, neither are your ways my ways," declares the Lord. "As the heavens are higher than the earth, so are my ways higher than your ways and my thoughts than your thoughts" (Isaiah 55:8-9).

That is how we live abundantly and in peace, knowing that He has

blessed us in the heavenly realms with every spiritual blessing in Christ (Ephesians 1:3b).

The Lord is just waiting to throw open the floodgates of the riches of heaven and pour out so many blessings we can't believe it! Now who would ever want to miss that!

Pray! Praying the Scriptures lifts us above our circumstances into His waiting arms.

LESSON 6

PRAYING THE SCRIPTURES

1.   Where is God in your circumstances?

2.   From Isaiah 9:6, what is the Lord to you?

3.   Why must your feelings be kept in check?

4.   How do you keep your faith bigger than your feelings?

5.   How do you keep yourself from being consumed with anxiety? Read verses and take notes.

6.   How do you keep yourself from worrying?

7.   How do you beat weariness (being emotionally tired)?

8.   What is the remedy for anger, bitterness, and a critical spirit?

9.   What do you do when you're discouraged or facing a crisis?

10. Where do you go for guidance when it seems impossible to face tomorrow?

11. What helps you in your loneliness?

12. Where do you find comfort in sorrow?

13.   How do you overcome temptation?

14.   What does praying Scripture do for you?

7

PRAYING DURING SPIRITUAL CONFLICT

One of the most essential times for us to pray is during spiritual conflict, yet we find that this is one of the most difficult times to pray. We have a tendency to withdraw inward and form a cocoon around ourselves when we are faced with conflict. And as a result, we isolate ourselves from our friends, from our loved ones, and most dangerously, from God. We could not be making a worse decision. For with that decision, we welcome Satan into our isolated shell. Satan is real. We briefly touched on him as the evil one in our study of the Lord's Prayer. One of Satan's goals is to keep us feeling defeated, discouraged, depressed, and confused as we wallow away in our spiritual conflict. Don't underestimate Satan, for he will do whatever it takes to accomplish his goals; and he has a lot of powerful allies who are willing to follow his evil bidding:

His tail swept a third of the stars out of the sky and flung them to earth.

He was hurled to the earth, and his angels with him (Revelation 12: 4a, 9b).

Satan has so many tricks up his sleeve, and he knows just how to use them to keep our focus off God, which will keep us in a spiritually weakened condition. For instance, have you ever thought about how he uses this subtle little trick to sidetrack our focus on God and to weaken us by wearing us down?

I truly wish I knew who wrote this article, "Too Busy," so I could thank them for opening my eyes to Satan's deceit. I only pray someday they are able to know how many lives they have kept from falling into Satan's grasp because of the truths they shared.

TOO BUSY[4]

Satan called a worldwide convention. In his opening address to his evil ones, he said, "We can't keep the Christians from going to church. We can't even keep them from conservative values. But we can do something else. We can keep them from forming a close, abiding relationship in Christ. If they gain that connection with Jesus, our power over them is broken. So let them go to church, let them have their lifestyles, but steal their *time*, so they can't gain that experience in Jesus Christ.

"This is what I want you to do, evil ones. Distract them from gaining hold of their Savior and maintaining that vital connection throughout their day!"

"How shall we do this?" shouted his evil followers.

"Keep them busy in the nonessentials of life, and invent things to occupy their minds," he answered. "Tempt them to spend, spend, spend, then borrow, borrow, borrow. Persuade the woman to work long hours and the men to work 6 or 7 days a week, 10 – 12 hours a day, so they can afford their lifestyles. Keep them from spending time with their children, because as their family fragments, their homes will soon offer no escape from the pressures of work.

"Over stimulate their minds so that they cannot hear that still small voice. Entice them to play the radio or cassette player whenever they drive, to keep the TV/VCR/CDs and their PCs going constantly in their homes. See to it that every store and restaurant in the world plays non-biblical, contradicting music constantly. This will jam their minds and break that union with Christ. Fill their coffee tables with secular magazines and newspapers. Pound their minds with the news 24 hours a day. Invade their driving moments with billboards. Flood their mailboxes with junk mail, sweepstakes, mail order catalogs, and every kind of newsletter and promotional offering free products, services, and false hopes.

"Even in their recreation, let them be excessive. Have them return from their recreation exhausted, disquieted, and unprepared for the coming week. Don't let them go out in nature to reflect on God's wonders. Send them to amusement parks, sporting events, concerts, and movies instead. And when they meet for spiritual fellowship, involve them in gossip and small talk so that they leave with troubled consciences and unsettled emotions. Crowd their lives with so many good causes that they have no time to seek power from Christ. Soon they will be working in their own strength, sacrificing their health and family for the good of the cause."

It was quite a convention in the end. The evil ones went eagerly to their assignments causing Christians everywhere to get busy, busy, busy and rush here and there. Satan's goal is to take our minds and hearts off Christ, then steer us toward the cares of the world. God wants us to enjoy life, but He must be first.

B	being
U	under
S	Satan's
Y	yoke

If we are too busy for God, then we are too busy!

Dandy little trick, huh? Oh, he's so good at it, too! Satan is constantly trying to confuse us so that we find it difficult to concentrate on God. He cannot tolerate our having a loving relationship with God. For your see, he considers God the Father his archenemy.

> *...he* [Jesus] *will crush your* [Satan's] *head,...*(Genesis 3:15c).

And Satan holds a big time grudge against Jesus.

> *And again, "I will put my trust in him." And again he says, "Here am I, and the children God has given me." Since the children have flesh and blood, he* [Jesus] *too shared in their humanity so that by his death he might destroy him who holds*

the power of death—that is, the devil—and free those who all their lives were held in slavery by their fear of death (Hebrews 2:13-15).

Satan's future is hopeless; his fate is sealed tighter than a drum, and he would love to convince you that your life is just as hopeless as his. Satan finds that task much easier to accomplish when we are distracted by our battle with spiritual conflict. He just sits back and watches as we try to do battle trusting our human feelings and depending upon our very limited human resources. When we fall into that trap, we <u>will</u> become convinced that our hope is gone. For as Satan knows, we don't have the capacity with our weak human arsenal to mount a successful offensive campaign, let alone a successful defensive one, to overcome the conflict.

But Satan also knows, and he hopes you don't (I pray you do!), that we have a vast reservoir of unlimited resources available to us that will renew our hope and enable us to come out the victor in our battle with spiritual conflict. Then Satan comes out the loser again. Are you interested in learning more about that reservoir and its resources? It is the heart of God. Join with me as we read, believe, and then receive these treasured nuggets of strength and hope straight from His heart to ours. Then let's store them into every nook and cranny of our hearts, and our hearts will be transformed into a treasure trove of hope. Hope in the One in whom we place our faith—our Father, Almighty God:

YOU SAY,
   GOD SAYS[5]

You say, "It's impossible."
God says, "All things are possible."

Jesus replied, "What is impossible with men is possible with God" (Luke 18:27).

You say, "I'm too tired."
God says, "I will give you rest."

"Come to me, all you who are weary and burdened, and I will give you rest. Take my yoke upon you and learn from me, for I am gentle and humble in heart, and you will find rest for your souls. For my yoke is easy and my burden is light" (Matthew 11:28-30).

You say, "Nobody really loves me."
God says, "I love you."

"For God so loved the world that he gave his one and only Son, that whoever believes in him shall not perish but have eternal life" (John 3:16).

"A new command I give you: Love one another. As I have loved you, so you must love one another" (John 13:34).

You say, "I can't go on."
God says, "My grace is sufficient."

But he said to me, "My grace is sufficient for you, for my power is made perfect in weakness." Therefore I will boast all the more gladly about my weaknesses, so

that Christ's power may rest on me
(2 Corinthians 12:9).

*"He will call upon me, and I will answer
him;*
I will be with him in trouble,
I will deliver him and honor him."
(Psalm 91:15).

You say, "I can't figure things out."
God says, "I will direct your steps."

Trust in the Lord with all your heart
and lean not on your own understanding;
in all your ways acknowledge him,
and he will make your paths straight
(Proverbs 3:5-6).

You say, "I can't do it."
God says, "You can do all things."

I can do everything through him who
gives me strength (Phil. 4:13).

You say, "I'm not able."
God says, "I am able."

And God is able to make all grace
abound to you, so that in all things at all
times, having all that you need, you will
abound in every good work
(2 Corinthians 9:8).

> *Now to him who is able to do immeasurably more than all we ask or imagine, according to his power that is at work within us,...* (Ephesians 3:20).

You say, "I can't forgive myself."
God says, "I forgive you."

> *If we confess our sins, he is faithful and just and will forgive us our sins and purify us from all unrighteousness* (1 John 1:9).

> *Therefore, there is now no condemnation for those who are in Christ Jesus,...* (Romans 8:1).

You say, "I can't manage."
God says, "I will supply all your needs."

> *And my God will meet all your needs according to his glorious riches in Christ Jesus* (Philippians 4:19).

You say, "I'm afraid."
God says, "I have not given you a spirit of fear."

> *For God did not give us a spirit of timidity, but a spirit of power, of love and of self-discipline* (2 Timothy 1:7).

You say, "I'm always worried and frustrated."
God says, "Cast all your cares on me."

> *Cast all your anxiety on him because he cares for you* (1 Peter 5:7).

You say, "I don't have enough faith."
God says, "I've given everyone a measure of faith."

> *For by the grace given me I say to every one of you: Do not think of yourself more highly than you ought, but rather think of yourself with sober judgment, in accordance with the measure of faith God has given you* (Romans 12:3).

You say, "I'm not smart enough."
God says, "I give you wisdom."

> *It is because of him that you are in Christ Jesus, who has become for us wisdom from God—that is, our righteousness, holiness and redemption* (1 Cor. 1:30).

> *If any of you lacks wisdom, he should ask God, who gives generously to all without finding fault, and it will be given to him* (James 1:5).

You say, "I feel all alone."
God says, "I will never leave you or forsake you."

> *"Never will I leave you; never will I forsake you"* (Hebrews 13:5b).

After having our hope renewed from pondering what "God Says" to us from His heart, is it any wonder that it just grinds Satan when we regain our focus on God? Satan simply cannot stomach it when he sees us down on our knees in prayer with God or sees us spending time in God's Word gaining spiritual strength. Spiritual conflict is no minor skirmish, it is a war, and Satan doesn't fight fair—for he has no conscience. But remember that when we pray and stay in God's Word, Satan doesn't think we fight fair, either. Because then he knows we are in direct communication with the One he can't fool by his trickery or defeat by his power. For Satan already took on God in battle and lost, and for his sinful effort he was unceremoniously thrown out of heaven.

> *"Through your widespread trade you were filled with violence, and you sinned. So I drove you in disgrace from the mount of God, and I expelled you, O guardian cherub, from among the fiery stones. Your heart became proud on account of your beauty, and you corrupted your wisdom because of your splendor. So I threw you to earth; I made a spectacle of you before kings"* (Ezekiel 28:16-17).

Satan now has a new battleground (this world) and a new focus for his battle plan (it's you and me). In order for us to fight the battle, we need a battle plan. The apostle Paul has laid out that plan for us. Paul understood what the war is about and how it should be fought. He fought it every day of his life, just like we must, after his conversion on the Damascus Road.

> *I know that nothing good lives in me, that is, in my sinful nature. For I have the desire to do what is good, but I cannot carry it out. For what*

*I do is not the good I want to do; no, the evil I do
not want to do—this I keep on doing. Now if I do
what I do not want to do, it is no longer I who do
it, but it is sin living in me that does it*
(Romans 7:18-20).

But he knew what strategy to use to fight his way out of
that predicament.

*And pray in the Spirit on all occasions
with all kinds of prayers and requests. With this
in mind, be alert and always keep on praying for
all the saints.*

*Pray also for me, that whenever I open
my mouth, words may be given me so that I will
fearlessly make known the mystery of the gospel,
for which I am an ambassador in chains. Pray
that I may declare it fearlessly, as I should*
(Ephesians 6:18-20).

I especially like verse 19. Paul knew how much he
needed prayer to be able to do what God had called him to do.
He also knew that every time he opened his mouth to speak, he
wanted it to be with words that were truthful, strong, and
fearless. Paul understood the fight—the natural human
tendencies that Satan wants us to dwell on, especially self-pity.
Paul certainly deserved one of the best pity parties ever. Just
read this:

*Are they Hebrews? So am I. Are they Israelites?
So am I. Are they Abraham's descendants? So
am I. Are they servants of Christ? (I am out of
my mind to talk like this.) I am more. I have
worked much harder, been in prison more*

frequently, been flogged more severely, and been exposed to death again and again. Five times I received from the Jews the forty lashes minus one. Three times I was beaten with rods, once I was stoned, three times I was shipwrecked, I spent a night and a day in the open sea, I have been constantly on the move. I have been in danger from rivers, in danger from bandits, in danger from my own countrymen, in danger from Gentiles; in danger in the city, in danger in the country, in danger at sea; and in danger from false brothers. I have labored and toiled and have often gone without sleep; I have known hunger and thirst and have often gone without food; I have been cold and naked (2 Corinthians 11:22-27).

To keep me from becoming conceited because of these surpassingly great revelations, there was given me a thorn in my flesh, a messenger of Satan, to torment me. Three times I pleaded with the Lord to take it away from me (2 Corinthians 12:7-8).

How easy for Paul to give up hope, to admit defeat, and to adapt the "woe is me" approach to life. How exactly did Paul respond? Read on:

But he said to me, "My grace is sufficient for you, for my power is made perfect in weakness." Therefore I will boast all the more gladly about my weaknesses, so that Christ's power may rest on me. That is why, for Christ's sake, I delight in weaknesses,   in   insults,   in   hardships,   in

persecutions, in difficulties. For when I am weak,
then I am strong (2 Corinthians 12:9-10).

By recognizing his own weaknesses, Paul knew that he had to reach out for the power to resist his human desires, and he knew he could reach that Power through PRAYER. He prayed, but he also asked for intercessory prayer from his loved ones (Ephesians 6:18-20).

Let's follow Paul's inspiring example of hope and faith by silencing our own pitiful, vain, and complaining babble, so that in the stillness of our soul we may listen to the still, small, and truthful voice of God. Remember, Satan lies. God <u>always</u> tells the truth. He will always make His presence known, and He will make it very clear to us that His strength is available when ours is zapped. Let's turn to the book of Daniel in the Old Testament for a vivid illustration of those points.

Daniel was a true man of prayer. He led an exemplary and trustworthy life, which was noticed by King Darius. The king chose Daniel to be a governmental administrator. In fact, Daniel's godly character was so visible that the king wanted to make Daniel the man in charge of the whole kingdom. Of course, that led to jealously, competition, and eventually the deadly plan by the other men involved to make sure Daniel did not achieve that position of power. Read about their scheme in Daniel 6:4-9:

> *At this, the administrators and the*
> *satraps tried to find grounds for charges against*
> *Daniel in his conduct of government affairs, but*
> *they were unable to do so. They could find no*
> *corruption in him, because he was trustworthy*
> *and neither corrupt nor negligent. Finally these*
> *men said, "We will never find any basis for*

charges against this man Daniel unless it has something to do with the law of his God."

So the administrators and the satraps went as a group to the king and said: "O King Darius, live forever! The royal administrators, prefects, satraps, advisers and governors have all agreed that the king should issue an edict and enforce the decree that anyone who prays to any god or man during the next thirty days, except to you, O king, shall be thrown into the lions' den. Now, O king, issue the decree and put it in writing so that it cannot be altered—in accordance with the laws of the Medes and Persians, which cannot be repealed." So King Darius put the decree in writing.

Even faced with the king's decree, Daniel would never bow down and pray to another god, or even to the king. Staying true to his heart's conviction, Daniel got on his knees and prayed to God three times a day. His so-called comrades couldn't wait to take this news to the king—their plan was working perfectly, so they thought. When King Darius heard this, he was greatly distressed, but to "save face" he had to follow through with his decree. But Daniel's making a stand for the honor of God and for the glory of God's name was a powerful witness. It reminds me of Paul's statement in Romans 1:16:

I am not ashamed of the gospel, because it is the power of God for the salvation of everyone who believes: first for the Jew, then for the Gentile.

That was so true of Daniel, and as a result, he made an impact on the pagan king.

> *So the king gave the order, and they brought Daniel and threw him into the lions' den. The king said to Daniel, "May your God, whom you serve continually, rescue you!" (Daniel 6:16.)*

The king had a sleepless night, to say the least, and at the light of dawn, he hurried to the lion's den.

> *When he came near the den, he called to Daniel in an anguished voice, "Daniel, servant of the living God, has your God, whom you serve continually, been able to rescue you from the lions?"*
>
> *Daniel answered, "O king, live forever! My God sent his angel, and he shut the mouths of the lions. They have not hurt me, because I was found innocent in his sight. Nor have I ever done any wrong before you, O king."*
>
> *The king was overjoyed and gave orders to lift Daniel out of the den. And when Daniel was lifted from the den, no wound was found on him, because he had trusted in his God* (Daniel 6:20-23).

What goes around comes around—you reap what you sow. Both phrases are often so true. The same men who plotted Daniel's death in this power grab, instead went to their own deaths, along with their families, in the same lion's den where Daniel had just safely spent the night.

> *At the king's command, the men who had falsely accused Daniel were brought in and thrown into the lion's den, along with their wives and children. And before they reached the floor of*

*the den, the lions overpowered them and crushed
all their bones* (Daniel 6:24).

Daniel prospered during the reign of Darius and the
reign of Cyrus. His testimony was known by many.

Read the <u>new</u> decree sent out by King Darius:

*Then King Darius wrote to all the
peoples, nations and men of every language
throughout the land:*

"May you prosper greatly!

*"I issue a decree that in every part of my
kingdom people must fear and reverence the God
of Daniel.*

*"For he is the living God and he endures
forever; his kingdom will not be destroyed, his
dominion will never end. He rescues and he
saves; he performs signs and wonders in the
heavens and on the earth. He has rescued Daniel
from the power of the lions."* (Daniel 6:25-27).

Daniel, through prayer and a deep personal relationship
with God, was a light in this dark world. Jesus tells all of us to
be the same.

*"You are the light of the world. A city on a hill
cannot be hidden. Neither do people light a lamp
and put it under a bowl. Instead they put it on its
stand, and it gives light to everyone in the house.
In the same way, let your light shine before men,
that they may see your good deeds and praise
your Father in heaven"* (Matthew 5:14-16).

When we stay connected to God through prayer, there is an essence that comes out of us because of Him who is in us.

Isaiah tells us in chapter 61 that the Lord will

> ...*bestow on them* [us] *a crown of beauty instead of ashes, the oil of gladness instead of mourning, and a garment of praise instead of a spirit of despair* (v.3b).

We will also be called

> ...*oaks of righteousness* [a symbol of strength], *a planting of the Lord for the display of his splendor* (v.3c).

How do you like that? What a great look for us to possess inside and out! The Lord promises that if we remain in Him (John 15:4), everlasting joy will be ours! That joy is abundant life to the fullest now and gives us hope for what is to come.

Life isn't easy. Jesus never said it would be. But through Him, we've been given the eyes to see a glimpse of the future. We see the end of the story. Guess who wins?

> *And the devil, who deceived them, was thrown into the lake of burning sulfur, where the beast and the false prophet had been thrown. They will be tormented day and night for ever and ever* (Revelation 20:10).

> *Then I saw a new heaven and a new earth, for the first heaven and the first earth had passed away, and there was no longer any sea. I*

saw the Holy City, the new Jerusalem, coming down out of heaven from God, prepared as a bride beautifully dressed for her husband. And I heard a loud voice from the throne saying, "Now the dwelling of God is with men, and he will live with them. They will be his people, and God himself will be with them and be their God. He will wipe every tear from their eyes. There will be no more death or mourning or crying or pain, for the old order of things has passed away."

He who was seated on the throne said, "I am making everything new!" Then he said, "Write this down, for these words are trustworthy and true." (Revelation 21:1-5).

What a glorious way to live, and may I say without fear of spiritual conflict:

We win—we really win!

LESSON 7

PRAYING DURING SPIRITUAL CONFLICT

1.	When is it the most difficult time to pray? Why?

2.	What is one of Satan's goals for us?

3.	How do you fight back? What do you say? What does God say?

4.	Is spiritual conflict an ongoing battle?

5.	What was the apostle Paul's battle? (Romans 7:18-20). What was his battle plan? (Ephesians 6:18-20.)

6.	Can you give any proof that God tells the truth, the whole truth, and nothing but the truth? (Take into account what we discovered in Chapter 1 – Why Pray?).

7.	Read Daniel 6. What do you understand about the character of Daniel?

8.	Why did the king have a sleepless night?

9.	Do you have any personal proof that you do reap what you sow?

10.	What lasting effects do you think Daniel's experience had on his relationship with God and others?

11.   According to Isaiah 61, what can you put on to make you a light where you live?

12.   Who lives happily ever after?

(Praise the Lord right now!)

8

PRAYING WITH "ATTITUDE"

It's time for an attitude check! In this final chapter, let's reflect on how our study so far has helped us to recognize that our attitude does impact our prayer relationship with God.

Prayer is a gift! When properly tuned with the correct attitude, prayer is a powerful instrument. Through prayer we can produce melodious harmony between the gift giver—God—and the benefactors of His gift—you and me. All of our prayers are arranged and orchestrated under the direction of the Holy Spirit.

But you, dear friends, build yourselves up in your most holy faith and pray in the Holy Spirit (Jude: 20).

When I pray, I'm fortified, and when I don't, I'm weak. My weakened condition then leads to worry, stress, panic, and the feeling of being out of control. The solution is so simple. Why worry, stress, and panic, when you can pray?

Prayer is our lifeline for achieving stability in an unstable world. Prayer settles us down when life's circumstances are unsettling. During those times of unrest, our natural human tendencies pressure us to give up and toss in the towel. However, through prayer we receive encouragement and fortitude to walk on as we look forward in faith. Just a little reminder: He does listen. He does want to hear from us. He wants to share our joys and also wants to unburden us from our heavy loads.

> *I cry aloud to the Lord; I lift up my voice to the Lord for mercy. I pour out my complaint before him; before him I tell my trouble.*
>
> *When my spirit grows faint within me, it is you who know my way. In the path where I walk men have hidden a snare for me. Look to my right and see; no one is concerned for me. I have no refuge; no one cares for my life.*
>
> *I cry to you, O Lord; I say, "You are my refuge, my portion in the land of the living." Listen to my cry, for I am in desperate need; rescue me from those who pursue me, for they are too strong for me. Set me free from my prison, that I may praise your name. Then the righteous will gather about me because of your goodness to me* (Psalm 142).

Prayer develops spiritual maturity. Prayer deepens our personal relationship with Almighty God, keeping our spiritual journey alive and exciting. Just think, God actually waits for us with the "Light" on in the living room of each of our hearts because He so desires to spend time with us right where we live. If we, in turn, desire to spend time with Him, we will find Him monitoring, directing, and instructing us regardless of the circumstances in which we find ourselves. He wants to remind us again and again of who He is and what He is capable of doing in and through us. Does His light that radiates through you to others reveal a spiritual attitude that honors the Light giver? Prayer affects our attitude, and we wear that attitude every waking minute of every day. What happens to our attitude when we pray with words such as these from Psalm 51 (selected verses)?

> *Have mercy on me, O God, according to your unfailing love; according to your great compassion blot out my transgressions* (v.1).

> *Wash away all my iniquity and cleanse me from my sin* (v.2).

> *Against you, you only, have I sinned and done what is evil in your sight, so that you are proved right when you speak and justified when you judge* (v.4).

> *Surely you desire truth in the inner parts; you teach me wisdom in the inmost place* (v.6).

> *Create in me a pure heart, O God, and renew a steadfast spirit within me* (v.10).

> *Restore to me the joy of your salvation and grant me a willing spirit, to sustain me* (v.12).

> *The sacrifices of God are a broken spirit; a broken and contrite heart, O God, you will not despise* (v.17).

That's what I call an attitude adjustment!

Prayer reveals His purpose for our lives. Because of His immeasurable love, He wants to change us through the channel of prayer. He wants to open our hearts and minds so we can recognize and then desire His will and His plan for our lives. He wants us to be like Jesus in every thought we think, every word we say, and every action we take. Yes, prayer can do all of that, for flowing through the channel of prayer is the Living Water:

> *On the last and greatest day of the Feast, Jesus stood and said in a loud voice, "If anyone is thirsty, let him come to me and drink. Whoever believes in me, as the Scripture has said, streams of living water will flow from within him"* (John 7:37-38).

> *"The Lord will guide you always; he will satisfy your needs in a sun-scorched land and will strengthen your frame. You will be like a well-watered garden, like a spring whose waters never fail."* (Isaiah 58:11).

Then our hearts are transformed as beautiful blossoms of personal, and most importantly, spiritual satisfaction and contentment spring forth.

He deserves to have our transformed hearts devoted to Him. Hearts that are truly devoted to God cannot and will not be restrained from worshiping Him with the praise and adoration only He deserves.

> *Therefore, I urge you, brothers, in view of God's mercy, to offer your bodies as living sacrifices, holy and pleasing to God—this is your spiritual act of worship* (Romans 12:1).
> *Praise the Lord.*
> *Praise God in his sanctuary; praise him in his mighty heavens.*
> *Praise him for his acts of power; praise him for his surpassing greatness.*

Praise him with the sounding of the trumpet, praise him with the harp and lyre, praise him with tambourine and dancing, praise him with the strings and flute, praise him with the clash of cymbals, praise him with resounding cymbals.

Let everything that has breath praise the Lord.

Praise the Lord (Psalm 150).

Having our hearts devoted to the Lord is the best way we can say thank you to Him. Our praise and adoration from the very depths of our hearts prove that our devotion is genuine. Our worship of Him proves that we humbly acknowledge that our proper position is to be on bended knee before the throne of the Almighty One. What a beautiful, yet humble, picture of praying with the right attitude.

Humility is a gorgeous trait that can only be possessed by the unaware. Humility keeps us in awe of God and the amazing love He has for us. Jesus was teaching His disciples a lesson on this very subject when He told them this parable (an earthly story with a heavenly meaning).

To some who were confident of their own righteousness and looked down on everybody else, Jesus told this parable: "Two men went up to the temple to pray, one a Pharisee and the other a tax collector. The Pharisee stood up and prayed about himself: 'God, I thank you that I am not like other men—robbers, evildoers, adulterers—or even like this tax collector. I fast twice a week and give a tenth of all I get.'

"But the tax collector stood at a distance. He would not even look up to heaven, but beat

*his breast, and said, 'God, have mercy on me, a
sinner.'*

*"I tell you that this man, rather than the
other, went home justified before God. For
everyone who exalts himself will be humbled,
and he who humbles himself will be exalted"*
(Luke 18:9-14).

When we are humble before God we will never be
confident in our own self-righteousness, because we know that
is not even possible. Only when we see ourselves the way we
really are, confess our sins before Him, and experience the joy
of a sinner set free, do we realize what His righteousness means.
We cannot make ourselves right before God—only Jesus can do
that. Then He raises us to a position of worth in God's eyes and
gives us freedom from guilt. That's exhilarating! Our souls
should then burst forth with thanksgiving and praise
(Psalm 145: selected verses).

*I will exalt you, my God the King; I will
praise your name for ever and ever. Every day I
will praise you and extol your name for ever and
ever.*

*Great is the Lord and most worthy of
praise; his greatness no one can fathom* (v.1-3).

*They will speak of the glorious splendor of your
majesty, and I will meditate on your wonderful
works* (v.5).

*The Lord is gracious and compassionate, slow to
anger and rich in love* (v.8).

*All you have made will praise you, O
Lord; your saints will extol you. They will tell of
the glory of your kingdom and speak of your
might, so that all men may know of your mighty
acts and the glorious splendor of your kingdom.
Your kingdom is an everlasting kingdom, and
your dominion endures through all generations.
The Lord is faithful to all his promises
and loving toward all he has made* (v.10-13).

His goodness and steadfast love endures forever! He
renews! He rebuilds! He restores! He will never forget us! He
engraves us on the palms of His hands!

*"Can a mother forget the baby at her breast and
have no compassion on the child she has borne?
Though she may forget, I will not forget you!
See, I have engraved you on the palms of my
hands; your walls are ever before me"*
(Isaiah 49:15-16).

Oswald Chambers said it this way, "The basis of prayer
is not what it costs us, but what it cost God to enable us to
pray."[6]

What a day that is going to be
When we actually see
Those scars from the nails Jesus bore at Calvary.
For then our eyes will see
What our hearts knew to be,
That Jesus loves you and me!

God is far more interested in a love relationship with you than He is in what you can <u>do</u> for Him. So,

> *Devote yourselves to prayer, being watchful and thankful* (Colossians 4:2).

<u>Devote</u> yourselves to prayer. Yes, it will take time, discipline, commitment, and self-sacrifice. But what you will receive will far exceed what you gave. Prayer was God's beautiful idea because He loves us. He knew it could and would change our hearts.

As our study comes to a close, let's approach His throne with an attitude of thanksgiving for the precious gift of His Son Jesus Christ, our Lord and Savior. And with our hearts joined together as one under the direction of the Holy Spirit, let's lift up to heaven on high our praise and adoration to honor and glorify Almighty God, who alone is the Power Source that makes

PRAYER—THE HEART CHANGER
AND MOUNTAIN MOVER.

Let's pray:

Almighty God,

We come with humbled hearts before Your throne. We see You high and exalted, worthy of worship.

Thank You for seeing us as pure and blameless, only because You see us through the cleansing blood of Your precious Son.

Thank You for loving us so much that You give us Truth—only truth. And may the truth of these pages sink into our hearts and show itself in our every thought, word, and deed, so that our lives will be living testimonies of Your life-changing goodness to everyone around us.

May we be forever connected with You, our God.

In our Savior's Name, we pray,

Amen.

LESSON 8

PRAYING WITH "ATTITUDE"

1. Why does our attitude need to be checked when we pray?

2. What will prayer do for you? What will prayer produce in you?

3. How does prayer affect your attitude when you pray Psalm 51?

4. How does prayer affect your attitude when you pray Psalm 150?

5. What is the best way to thank the Lord for what He has done for you?

6. Read Luke 18:9-14. Explain humility.

7. How does prayer affect your attitude when you pray Psalm 145:1-13?

8. How long will the Lord's goodness and love for you last?

9. How do we know that the Lord will never forget us? (Isaiah 49:15-16.)

10.   What did it cost God to enable us to pray? Does that affect you in any way? How? Why?

11.   How do you <u>know</u> that God loves you?

12.   Read Colossians 4:2. What does "devote" mean?

Now it's up to you.
Give prayer a chance to change your heart
and to move a mountain.

ACKNOWLEDGEMENTS

For permission to reprint copyrighted material, grateful acknowledgement is made to the following publishers:

HOLY BIBLE: NEW INTERNATIONAL VERSION®. NIV®. Copyright © 1973, 1978, 1984 by International Bible Society. Used by permission of The Zondervan Corporation.

HOLY BIBLE: NEW KING JAMES VERSION, NKJV, Copyright© 1982 by Thomas Nelson, Inc. Used by permission. All rights reserved.

"Trust His Heart." Causing Change Music/Dayspring Music (administered Dayspring Music, LLC), copyright© 1989. All rights reserved. Used by permission.

REFERENCES

1. Random House Webster's Unabridged Dictionary, Second Edition ©1997, 1996, 1993, 1987 by Random House, Inc. All rights reserved.

2. Eddie Carswell and Babbie Mason, "Trust His Heart." Copyright 1989 Causing Change Music/Dayspring Music (administered Dayspring Music, LLC). All rights reserved. Used by permission.

3. Spafford, Horatio G. and Philip P. Bliss, "It Is Well With My Soul."

4. Author Unknown. "Too Busy."

5. Author Unknown. "You Say, God Says" format.

6. Oswald Chambers, The Best from All His Books, chosen and edited by Harry Verploegh. Oliver Nelson: A division of Thomas Nelson Publishers.